DECODE
Tarot

DEBRA ZACHAU

DECODE
Tarot

Master Meanings, Reversals, and Combinations

REDFeather™
MIND | BODY | SPIRIT

Library of Congress Control Number: 2024931491

Cover Image: Shutterstock Labyrinth
Type set in Playbill/Fenice

ISBN: 978-0-7643-6806-6
Printed in India

Published by REDFeather Mind, Body, Spirit
An imprint of Schiffer Publishing, Ltd.
4880 Lower Valley Road
Atglen, PA 19310
Phone: (610) 593-1777; Fax: (610) 593-2002
Email: Info@redfeathermbs.com
Web: www.redfeathermbs.com

For our complete selection of fine books on this and related subjects, please visit our website at www.redfeathermbs.com. You may also write for a free catalog.

REDFeather Mind, Body, Spirit's titles are available at special discounts for bulk purchases for sales promotions or premiums. Special editions, including personalized covers, corporate imprints, and excerpts, can be created in large quantities for special needs.
For more information, contact the publisher.

FSC
www.fsc.org
MIX
Paper from
responsible sources
FSC® C016779

I dedicate this to Susanna.

Thank you with all my heart.

—Debra

CONTENTS

PART TWO *Master the Courts*

PART THREE *Master the Majors*

The purpose of this book is to educate and empower. I do not guarantee that anyone following these techniques, suggestions, tips, ideas, or strategies will achieve particular results. However, if guidelines are followed, chances for success are increased. I shall have neither liability nor responsibility with respect to any loss or damage caused or alleged to be caused directly, or indirectly, by the information contained in this collection of work.

Even though this book does not teach medical intuition, some in this field may find the techniques helpful in understanding root health issues. That being said, I must mention here that this book in all of its various mediums does not replace the advice of a medical professional. Consult your physician before making any changes to your diet or regular health plan.

I take all facets of the psychic sciences seriously; the information in this book is subjective and has proven to work very well, not only for myself but for many of my students. All the information in this book is from my perspective and given to better help the psychic community as a whole become more accurate and continue to up-level the integrity of our work—all for entertainment purposes. To be clear, every Tarot card has the same general customary description and isn't owned by any one author. It's owned by the historical craft. Therefore, the basic meanings I provide for each card are from a universal understanding and will not be cited back to any one author. Wording may appear the same; however, there are only a few descriptive words available to ensure accuracy of lineage so that they stay sound and viable throughout the generations. I created this book without the use of AI. Not one word.

Debra Zachau
https://debrazachau.com/
growyourlight.com training.growyourlight.com
Tarot video course

❶
Introduction

Tarot has so much to tell you about yourself, others, and the world. It can provide a gateway to sharing information from loved ones who have passed, or it can enable you to have a nice chat with your animals. Knowing the basic meanings of each card and then understanding the frame of reference the readings are focused on can give you volumes of information.

There are two kinds of people in the world: people who are discovering themselves and people who are remembering themselves. One isn't better or more talented than the other, but the way they learn is different. Discovering and exploring your intuition and metaphysical tools for the first time is exciting and new. Someone discovering how Spirit communicates and providing such a blast of understanding all at once may overwhelm them and take awhile for them to know what to do next.

Most of the people attracted to my work are remembering themselves. They will grow fond of certain cards whose message travels straight from their spirit council in ways that can't be explained. One or two cards can trigger memories and wisdom they can't explain—they know—and their guidance as advisors can be remarkable.

Decode Tarot: Master Meanings, Reversals, and Combinations concentrates on the three areas in the Tarot that trigger those memories and innate wisdom, addressing not only the meaning of each card but the combinations, crossings, and reversals. There can be a spontaneous awareness of what needs to be said, and using the Tarot as a guide ensures that you stay inside your intuition and not drift into imagination.

Master the Minors, Majors, and Courts chapters reveal the profound insight to bring the puzzle together and provide the Aha! moments you have been searching for on your journey toward understanding. Isn't that what we are all searching for? Someone who can share the right combination of words to make sense of everything? You can be that for another person through the Tarot. It will provide you with the right combination of words to bless someone in their hour of need. Words can lift their burden by repositioning their attachment to it to a better place of understanding—a safe place that will provide the client with enough insight to know their next steps. Not just to try something, but to know a situation so well that insecurity isn't a bother anymore.

All the combinations have been tested and are *my* secret language of the Tarot that I am sharing with you. This secret will save you years of diligent note-taking and follow-up inquiries. Each combination following the specific card explanation shows vetted examples that have stood the test of time through thousands of readings. I test my card combinations to make sure they make sense in many different situations. The messages must be clear and include some sort of follow-up, needed to test the accuracy.

One single card is not a complete reading, because each card you lay down tells more of the story. For instance, if you have an ace of any suit, it will always mean the beginning of something. The element of the suit will tell you the energetic signature of that beginning, but the next card or cards after that will tell you more of the specifics. For instance, the Ace of Wands means the beginning of an action, and the cards you lay down after that ace will tell you what direction your action should go in. For example, if the suit of Pentacles comes next, you can advise that the action needs to be tangible and materialistic: buying, selling, someone. The answers are always in the cards. This book will help you see and hear the correct messages the Tarot intends to share.

There are two important parts to a Tarot deck: the Major Arcana and the Minor Arcana. Arcana means "mysteries." There are 56 minor cards dedicated to everyday life and 22 major cards dedicated to the higher perspectives of life. The minor cards highlight the mundane, everyday events and people in your life, and the major cards give voice to the angels, guardians, and guides. Information given in the major cards can, energetically, back you up far enough from a difficult situation to understand why something is happening and what the best solutions may be from the perspective of ethics, morals, and spiritual principles. The minor cards talk about the daily events and the people who influence your experience.

It's important to remember that a person is never bound by these predictions. An advisor reads the client's energy signature or the signature of the client's person of interest. All psychics read and understand the future this way. Inside that river of energy lives focus points and impulses. The Tarot will explain how strong those impulses are within that framework, and bring understanding and direction.

It would look like this: if I'm asked, "Is my girlfriend missing me or thinking about me?," I would be able to first see if she is indeed thinking about him, and, after that, evaluate how strong her impulses are to pick up the phone and call or reach out in some other way. If perhaps I see hesitation on her end but see (by looking at a line of cards) a sweet melancholy about her regarding him, I would encourage my client to reach out first because his efforts will, most likely, be welcomed.

We often have impulses to call someone but may be overwhelmed by distractions, and the Tarot will show this as well. When those impulses come, they don't always rise to the level of action. Knowing the most probable future can give you an idea of what a person can do to influence that probable future and lean toward their desired outcome. It's fascinating and, most of all, enlightening!

The Minor Arcana are the numbered cards, similar to playing cards; they rank ace through 10. These cards represent everyday matters. They encompass small to large annoyances and turmoil as well as joyful experiences in store for us. These cards tell you how long a phase will last in your life if no new choices are made. Inside the Minor Arcana is a set of 16 cards known as the Court cards or the family, as I like to refer to them. These cards represent the people in your life: your father, mother, sisters and brothers, friends and bosses—everyone who can either lift you or block and restrict you.

People are represented as Kings, Queens, Knights, and Pages. Each has their personality, as defined by their specific suit. Each suit has certain traits (as will be explained in depth), and each person represented in the Court cards will have a unique disposition of their particular suit.

You will learn the basics about these family cards in the first part of the book, but a deeper dive into the people in your life is provided in part 2, "Master the Courts." That detail is sure to provide a solid relationship between you and each of the 16 personalities, and you can confidently advise others with just a glance of any Court card.

A note about reading for yourself: the reason so many advisors caution against it is because you, as the reader, are so biased. Also, I've discovered that the throw will reflect how you're feeling about the situation and not give you a solution to the problem. Here is the reason why. If someone is really upset about something or suspects someone in their life of doing something, and they do a throw for themselves with all the cards being positive cards, the reader will not believe the message of happiness. They will think that none of the cards reflect how they feel, or meet them where they are, so they can't trust the message. If a reader doesn't feel that the cards understand their situation (and of course, in their mind and heart it's tragic), they will dismiss the reading altogether. To avoid this, try to be as unbiased as you can while shuffling. Better yet, call a colleague; have them throw a message on your behalf.

To sum up, I appreciate the craft, the amount of professionalism needed for excellence, and how long it takes to build a language of insight to achieve favorable results. Students need bravery, even boldness, to share this insight, as well as a discipline to take that information and decipher it into a deliverable product that's understandable, concise, and actionable. *Decode Tarot* is a master class for personal and professional success in the psychic sciences. *The Clarity Tarot* deck, also published by REDFeather, was designed for advisors who were very busy on the psychic hotlines or in private practice. Because there are keywords on each card, this deck is also perfect for the beginner. *Decode Tarot* takes you from reading upright only along with traditional meanings into specific combinations, crosses, and reversals that have proved accurate by testing them over thousands of readings and client feedback.

PART ONE
Master the Minors

❷
MASTERING THE MINORS

First, please take a look at your deck to make sure the box has the word "Tarot" and not "Oracle." There are two types of divination decks, and they get mixed up a lot. An oracle deck has an undefined amount of cards. Oracle cards may have pictures and words, or just words. There can be as few as 20 cards to well over 100, with each acting as a trigger, or prompt, for the reader to open their minds to information that may be available. A traditional Tarot deck will always have 78 cards. Those cards will have four suits that carry specific traits and personalities. Each number represents a clue, signal, or prompt for the reader to adjust their energy to receive messages for themselves or their clients.

Next, separate your deck into the different sections. Take the 22 Major cards out and set them aside. These are the Fool, Magician, High Priestess, Empress, Emperor, Hierophant, Lovers, Chariot, Strength, Hermit, Wheel of Fortune, Justice, Hanged Man (sometimes called Hanging Man), Death, Temperance, Devil, Tower, Star, Moon, Sun, Judgment, and World cards.

Then, separate the four sets of the Court cards. They are the King, Queen, Knight, and Page of Wands, Swords, Cups, and Pentacles.

Last, what you have left should be four stacks of cards: Ace through 10 of Wands, Ace through 10 of Swords, Ace through 10 of Cups, and Ace through 10 of Pentacles.

As a sidenote, some Tarot decks have rebranded the suits into their elements. For instance, Pentacles may be called Coins or Earth because pentacles represent the material world. Pentacles are represented in regular playing cards as Diamonds (earth element). Wands may be labeled Fire, Scepters, or Rods and represented in playing cards as Clubs (fire element). Swords have the element of air and sometimes are referred to in Tarot decks as Thoughts, Blades, Knives; anything sharp can represent this suit. It refers to a sharp mind and sharp and smart communication skills. Our voice travels through air waves and is a good way to remember the deeper meaning of this suit. Not surprisingly, Swords are represented in the playing-card deck as Spades. Last but not least is the suit of Cups, which is a water element. Cups represent our emotions, and our emotions are what influence us to action. In a deck of playing cards they are represented by the suit of Hearts. Other names for this suit could be Water, Caldrons, and Chalices.

THE SUITS AND THEIR PERSONALITIES

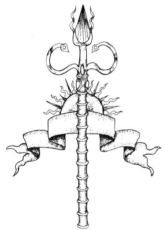

The Suit of Wands

Take a look at the Wands stack first. You may notice that the primary element for this suit is fire. Most decks will illustrate that at one or both ends of the wand. This is the symbol for quick action. Easy to remember because if you put your hand near the fire, you will pull it back fast without thinking, right? If perhaps you are doing a reading and many of the cards are from the suit of Wands, you will know that the problem or the solution (or both) comes in the form of action. The stories of anger, rage, races, punching, air travel, driving, biking, walking, or running away (or toward, for that matter) will be told through the suit of Wands.

If there was a horse race with four horses running, each bearing the name of one suit, the Wands' horse would certainly come in first by a mile. When people talk about the energy of a card or a reading of a suit, it means we note the speed of manifestation. The personality of this suit means there is little time between thought and actions. Have you ever sat down to write a story or create a piece of art, and everything comes together? When all the words you write are perfect, and the story needs very little editing, or the painting is created in minutes and not hours, that's fast action. Have you ever walked into a meeting at work to do a presentation and, in the middle of it, you notice your audience is listening, transfixed by every word and concept? Success is measured from beginning to end in a few minutes, seconds even.

The shadow side of this "energy" is when you feel moved to anger, and no matter how much you try not to speak, the momentum of the situation seems to force you into it. The words that hurt instead of heal spill out, leaving you needing to somehow move past your pride to find a way to reconcile.

Much of the hustle and bustle of the world is an example of the Wands suit bringing pressure for people to hurry faster than they should. The bottom line is that the presence of many Wand cards in a reading should inspire the advisor to tell the client to be mindful of quick action and speech and to hold on, since the bounty of all good things can bloom quickly if you remain mindful.

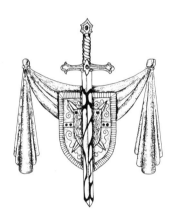

The Suit of Swords

The next-fastest horse in this energetic race is the suit of Swords, with the element of air. This is the suit of the curiosity-driven, mediators, and debate enthusiasts. This horse comes in second because overthinking can cause you to second-guess, check things over and over, and worry about the "what ifs" in life. When you are aware of its benefits, you can ride the wave of inspiration and epiphanies and revel in the joy of quick wit and perfect conclusions.

In a reading with many Sword cards, you can be sure your client has been mulling things over in their heads. Overthinking can dull the normally sharp edge of your mind. The shadow side of this suit, simply put, is when your words harm instead of heal. This suit is so very smart and can outthink the best in any group, but if anger is behind the action, there will be hurt feelings for sure.

The Suit of Cups

The energy of the Cups suit is water, emotion, and intuition of all measures. Air (Swords) with thoughts, fire (Wands) with action, and water (Cups) for how we feel about all those thoughts and actions.

Revisiting our horse race, we will find the speed of our Cups horse much, much slower than the first two. In fact, horses 1 and 2, Wands and Swords, have already crossed the finish line and are having champagne in the stable before this emotionally charged horse crosses the line. Why so slow? That's an easy answer: our emotions will cause us to pause every chance they get. Sadness is so heavy. When we feel sad or are supporting another while they're sad, we pace ourselves slower. Like water itself, it needs firm boundaries to be held in one place. The ridged walls of the glass or rocks on the shore hold that water safe inside.

If given liberty, melancholy-type emotions can spill over and slow us down. If blessed with spontaneous joy, we become distracted and off-balance. The blessing of the Cups is empathy, the ability to understand another person's emotional state. If you have an insight into how they got to their difficult situation, you, as an advisor, will be able to shepherd them out of the confusion.

The Suit of Pentacles

We are left now with the slowest horse in our race. The horse is named Pentacles. Why so slow? Because this poor guy is dragging the house, the car, the relationships, and the job—not to mention the retirement fund and savings accounts—behind it. The energy is earth, and the earth is dense. When doing a reading with lots of Pentacles or coins, things can be slow to manifest.

I once did a reading that illustrates this so well. The client wanted to know about starting her own business. The cards were so clear, a person wouldn't have had to know the meaning of each card to know the answer for her. There were Sword cards at the beginning of the reading and Wand cards right after that, indicating that she had the idea (Swords) for business, then took action (Wands) by already applying for the loan. Dotted in and around both these suits were mixed emotions (Cups), showing both excitement and worry. But near the end of this particular lineup of cards were Pentacles, meaning that her thoughts, actions, and emotions together were headed for success.

I like to say that Pentacles are the only grounded cards because the energy of Wands, Swords, and Cups lives aboveground and is constantly in flux. The lineup of cards in a reading is called a throw or spread. Specifically, several cards are placed on the table faceup or facedown, depending on how you like to read. I prefer throwing my cards faceup because, as I see each card, a story unfolds and it suggests how to talk to the client.

A Word about Spreads

There are many spreads, and they serve a good purpose. A spread is a patterned layout: you place the cards into where every spot a card lands in the spread has a meaning attached. For instance, the Celtic Cross is one of the most popular spreads and my favorite. This 10-card throw breaks each card down to a specific part and place in a person's life. It is used by many practitioners because it gives so much information in a single throw.

1. The first card symbolizes the situation or topic.

2. The second card is what is crossing or possibly the cause of the trouble in your client's life.

3, 4, 5. The third, fourth, and fifth cards tell you what your client feels on the inside (about the situation), and what event or energy happened just prior to the reading to influence the current situation.

6. The sixth card represents the most probable next steps your client will make prior to your counsel.

7. The seventh card is how the client feels about themselves.

8. The eighth card speaks about the client's environment, which includes work as well as home.

9. The ninth card is the place that reveals the client's hopes and dreams, basically telling you if the client has a positive or negative feeling about the situation.

10. The tenth card gives you an idea of how things will be turning out. This is the most probable future if no change is made.

④
REVERSALS, COMBINATIONS, SHUFFLING, AND TIMING

Reversals

It is often assumed that a reversed card means the opposite or is worse than the upright meaning. That isn't always the case, so be careful. The reversed Five of Cups is a bit better than the upright. The upright meaning is guilt and remorse through a disappointment, while the reverse means you aren't sure how to handle this disappointment and are leaning away from the hurt. Both mean emotional pain, but in different ways. The Death card upright indicates a complete natural ending with a fresh start on something new, while the reverse means you are having a hard time letting go of something that won't work out. So when you have a reverse card, it doesn't necessarily mean the situation will get worse.

Combinations

I explain not only what each card means but combinations of cards that I have discovered to be right on when predicting the future or evaluating a confusing situation. When providing a reading to someone who is in crisis, it's important to be able to clearly define, and mirror back, the client's perspective. This makes the person feel confident that you know how and why they feel the way they do. I'm not saying their perspective is the best one for the situation at hand. That is for the cards and Spirit to define, but understanding how your client is processing information and being able to verbalize that will prove successful. To be clear, the meanings of the cards are the same whether you learn them here or in another book or video. The Two of Swords will always mean the same thing, regardless of the Tarot deck or book. It is where the card sits in a reading that provides the road map and understanding.

Shuffling

I suggest you shuffle the cards as they organically move on and off the table and into your hands. Don't waste time turning all the cards upright before shuffling; just shuffle and throw down your reading. Before turning the reversals upright, take a moment and ask yourself if Spirit is recommending I read these cards as blocks to happiness. Maybe a reversal can mean someone is blinded to the obvious? It's all good information. Some cards on the table will be information just for *you*, on how to advise the client, and some cards will be information for you to tell the client. Understanding the difference will make you an outstanding counselor.

Timing

I never waiver from a one-month format and assign 30 days to each card. As a professional advisor, you will be asked to predict a minute-by-minute scenario. I don't play the minute game, and neither should you. The future is always in flux, on the basis of the actions people take in each moment; life doesn't manifest in a straight line. My predictions and trajectories will go in and out of probability often, and offering tight time frames is risky. The event or situation coming around will be within about 30 days. Remind your client that life can give or take a couple of weeks either way. Stay fluid. An example is this: When will my client meet someone new? There is a line of cards in front of me to answer the question. The third card from the left is the **Ace of Cups (new passion).** I would say, "It looks like within three months," then encourage them to accept all invitations to be social with others. (This isn't the only way I read timing, just an example of how you can do a quick calculation to answer the question.) Polish up your dating profile and say yes to a get-together after work for a drink. Even if you stay only a few minutes, the action forward with the anticipation of meeting someone makes you a magnet for attracting what you desire. I do tell my clients that action can quicken a timeline prediction. To be clear, I match one card with a 30-day measure, noting that the event can happen *anytime* inside that time frame.

5

ACE OF WANDS

(New Action)

ACE of WANDS.

Since our Wand suit has the element of fire and fast-moving energy, when you see the Ace of Wands you know there is a call to *physical* action of some kind. This is the beginning of the exercise program, project of interest, and spontaneous race to the mailbox. This is an active inspiration for creativity. Just for the record, and I will be mentioning this again, anytime you see an Ace from any of the four suits, it's always good news! Aces represent the beginning of something. **Ace of Wands** is about **new action. Ace of Swords** is a new *idea*. **Ace of Cups** shows **new** *emotions* bringing new perspectives. Finally, **Ace of Pentacles** heralds the beginning of new *income*, fame, fortune, or standing in a community.

Ace of Wands (new action) close to the **6 of Cups (family and long-ago past)** suggests reconnecting to the past in some way, a phone call or reunion. If the client is asking about money and career, it could mean an old friend from childhood, or a family member will help with finding work or starting a business. The same group of people may introduce you to someone to start a love relationship if that is the frame of reference. I have found that the 6 of Cups brings in conversations and reconnections with people from times as far back as elementary school, and vital people you enjoyed growing up.

The **Ace of Wands (new action)** paired with the **10 of Swords (feeling betrayed**; this card, being a 10, closes a cycle). Can mean the business partnership or romance may start unbelievably strong, burn hot, then burn out. If this ace (or any ace, for that matter), is followed by **Death (complete and natural end of a cycle)**, it means about the same thing, only with less drama. The couple in work or romance will be in agreement that things were fun, but it feels like the business or love option simply isn't a match, and both go about their day happy to have met a new friend. There are ways to tweak the above combination with grace, however, while being honest yet kind with your client. Here is how I would do this: Let's say the client came in and wants to know if the person she just met will feel like starting a relationship with her. I look at the future through his eyes for that answer, not hers (I already know she is interested in a positive outcome from this date). Let's say the cards show this **Ace of Wands (new action)** and the **Death card (natural endings)** after that. I would say to my client, "When looking through his eyes, I see he isn't looking for anything serious or permanent at this time. Feelings and directions can change, of course, but please don't spend a lot of thought and emotional currency hoping for something substantial from this person. At least not for now. Then I would remind my client that my readings go out in one-month increments and only for a few months. He could change his mind after getting to know you better, but don't hand your heart over to him too soon. In the meantime, go out and have fun with him; just stop when he wants to become intimate when the security of exclusivity hasn't been discussed yet.

Ace of Wands (new action) with the **3 of Pentacles (apprentice, good at work)** predicts new work that's fulfilling regarding job/career, and positive actions to anchor relationship, whether the subject is love or money.

Ace of Wands (new action) with the **High Priestess (intuition and spiritual thought)** or **Hierophant (traditional religious influence)** looks like new actions toward either learning or teaching on topics of a spiritual nature. If reading about job or career, it suggests success when pursuing a job or project that aligns with morals and ethics. I find this most often when someone has an impulse to do community work. When you're talking about love, it speaks of a spiritual connection with your person of interest, and the upright Hierophant means both are not afraid of marriage.

Are you beginning to see how one card influences the other? How the Ace of Wands suggests the beginning of action, but the following cards will tell you in what area? Here are a few more that I have found to be correct every time they show up. I have tested these combinations by doing thousands of readings and asking clients for clarification.

Ace of Wands (new action) with the **8 of Wands (very fast-moving energy; both are in the wand family)** plus a more negative card such as perhaps the **Devil (obsessive/compulsive)** or the **Moon reversed (hidden agenda)** or **Magician reversed (manipulation)**. Here I would advise my client to keep their eyes wide open and see through the haze of romance and point him to the door! Our Devil speaks of a controlling personality, and the Moon means your love interest is hiding something from you. When reading for job/career and you don't have an option not to take the job or quit an existing job, it suggests that they document everything, because someone is either taking credit for your work or sabotaging your progression in the company. Reversed Devil or Moon is always a bad actor, so keep your wits about you. If you are needing a job, make sure you check and recheck the contract, since what was negotiated in the interview may not make it to the final contract.

Ace of Wands (new action) and the **10 of Wands (uneven responsibilities)** means you will be doing all the heavy lifting in that job or relationship. A lopsided relationship or job that expects more from you than others. We never want to tell our clients what to do, only what to expect if plans remain the same. After all, they manifested it, and it's understandable they would be hesitant to walk away from the situation or newly formed relationship. Having a psychic reading that contains negative cards can shine the light on potential problems. Your client can then ask the right questions of their new love and not dismiss red flags. If the question is about career, this combination is a good reminder to get answers in writing before agreeing to a job. Readings like this regarding love are important to ensure that the client doesn't surrender their heart to someone before all the facts and expectations are clear.

Ace of Wands (new action) and the **Lovers (physical love and collaborations, with a focus on creation).** Look for a card after these two that will anchor the project or romance down. If perhaps the next few cards are more Wands, you can bet for business and pleasure the situation will burn hot and then burn out. If, on the other hand, you have the **Emperor (corporate structure)** or **7 of Pentacles (money grows slowly but steadily)**, that business deal should start and continue to prosper. For a love reading, I would like to see more Cups around that Lovers card. For romance, if the Lovers card stands alone, without the suit of Cups representing some emotion, then it's safe to believe that this may be a friend-with-benefits mentality, and that person being discussed is not looking for a healthy, progressive, and exclusive relationship at this time.

6

TWO OF WANDS

(Progressing Well)

The 2s always indicate partnerships and collaborations. Most often, the 2 of Wands presents a slow but positive forward motion with their chosen path. An all-around happy card. Progressing well toward partnerships of all kinds. The cards surrounding this will tell you in which field. For instance, if you have the **2 (collaboration)** of **Wands (action)** next to **Pentacles (the material)**, you can be sure it means partnering up with someone for a profit of some kind. **Cups (emotion)**, a relationship. **Swords (thoughts)**, debate, or coauthoring on a project. But because we are reading through the suit of actions, the other cards will tell you where that action will or should go.

Another example is the **2 of Wands (progressing well)** with the **7 of Swords (not trustworthy)**. This will give you caution about collaborating with this other person, whether it be business or personal relationships. The topic doesn't matter because it indicates someone around them wants to take something away.

In fact, if the **2 of Wands** is sitting next to any **negative cards**, you can be sure your progression will be stalled or, worse, sabotaged by another. Put the negative cards *before* the **2 of Wands (progressing well)**, and it says the project or relationship will ultimately smooth out.

Continuing with another example, the **2 of Wands (progressing well)** with **any Pentacle (finances, property, acquisitions)** and the **Devil (obsession/compulsions)** means an unbalanced situation or platform. Everything looks great (**2 of Wands and tangible partnership**) until somebody's bad habits or poor coping skills (**Devil**) slow the progression.

Replacing the **Devil** with the **High Priestess (spiritual/intuitions)** will mean the project or relationship may not be grounded enough to succeed on the anticipated timeline when talking about business.

The **High Priestess (spiritual/intuition)** sitting close to the **2 of Wands (progressive action)** in a relationship reading means the two people have discovered a thread of spiritual alignment that creates a magical feeling but does not mean the relationship is grounded in reality. It is an added value but doesn't translate to sensible thinking. Those lovely thoughts of love are floating in the land of wishes and unicorns. You will need to see a grounded card or rather serious card to bring the relationship or project out of dreamland and into reality.

The **2 of Wands (progressing well)** and the **2 of Cups (collaboration)** in a business reading could mean a cottage business where two people join together for profit or a family business. I've discovered that if there are Pentacles around this combination, it indicates meeting a person at work to start a romantic relationship or meeting a person who knows your industry well. Either way, this combination is fun and full of hope for the future.

The **2 of Wands (progressing well)** with the **3 of Swords (harsh words)** or **5 of Wands (gossip/bickering)** is a combination showing that nobody feels heard, and, in a career or business reading, progression will often stall. In a relationship reading, consider leaving or at the very least reclaim your heart. If you've already surrendered your heart and want to make it work, you may need to find professional help. Both need to have a deep desire to look at personal motives and intentions to find peace.

The **2 of Wands (progressing well)** coupled with **any Court card** will indicate that someone is helping or hindering your situation. If the Court card is **upright**, then it is a **helper** in the situation. If the Court card is **reversed**, then that person is **blocking** or sabotaging the situation. This is a case where a reversed Court card does have an opposite meaning.

❼
THREE OF WANDS

(Creativity, Trade, Commerce, Small Successes)

Most often, the image on this card is of a person looking out to the next horizon. Sometimes they are looking over land or calm water, which represents a progression of actions. It has been my experience that when the 3 of Wands appears in a love reading, it may mean the person of interest is in another country, travels for a living, or is communicating over the internet. To be clear, it doesn't always mean internet dating, but it does indicate something standing in the way. Usually, it is distance, literally physical mileage. Look to the other cards around this one to clarify the story. If perhaps there are Court cards in the suit of Swords, this person of interest may be in the military, law enforcement, or any industry where a formal uniform is worn. The discipline required for that kind of work may create a gap in smooth progression in relationships simply due to unusual hours and shifts. In a love reading, I relate this card as an indicator that there is a distance between the parties. Instead of mileage, it can be an unsupportive family or cultural differences keeping them apart. If a **reversed Court card (representing people in your life)** is close, it could mean a passed loved one has entered the reading with a message. In this case, the distance between each other is death itself and the veil separating us. For it to be a message through mediumship from a passed loved one, this reversed Court card will need to be close to this 3. The intended message from the passed loved one begins *after* the reversed Court. Unwavering faith in a life-after-life existence creates the avenues or portals that support the communication we all desperately crave here on Earth from our passed loved ones (more about mediumship readings later). The 3 of Wands can bring in a sense of melancholy and a longing for something faraway to return. For the most part, the 3 is a low number, bringing small successes. If this card is coupled with a Major Arcana card, it may indicate a bigger success, for instance:

The 3 of Wands **(small creative success)** together with one or more of these—**Wheel of Fortune (cycle of life)**, the **World (triumph)**, or **Emperor (financial corporations)**—could propel you to greater wins, adding a bit of luck to your original small success to make your project and efforts much bigger

The 3 of Wands **(small success)** together with one or more of these major cards, **Hermit (drawing inward)** or the **Hanging Man (stopping to look at things differently)**, will encourage you to slow down and rethink where you are going. This could be Spirit asking you to look around to make sure all the right components, papers, or ingredients are in the mix before going further.

The **Death card (natural ending)**: if it comes *before* the 3 of Wands, this will indicate you are still working on a project that has already provided all it can. If **Death** comes *after* the 3, it suggests you stop completely and not move forward. It may be asking you to abandon the project or relationship and walk away or stop investing for a few months. The rest of the card lineup will reveal more specifics.

The 3 of Wands **(small success)** with the 6 of Wands **(others notice your efforts)** points to a promotion or new information to propel you forward.

The 3 of Wands **(small success)** with the 7 of Cups **(not all options are rooted in reality)** means the project or relationship seems to offer many options, and not all of those options are viable. Read the fine print. As mentioned above, if this card is reversed or unfortunate (surrounded by negative cards), it can indicate progress stalling.

⑧
FOUR OF WANDS

(A Stable Foundation)

This is one happy card! The number 4 gives you strong foundations with focus leaning in traditional ways regarding both work and family. This indicates strong support building around you and is an especially welcome card that uplifts neighboring cards. There is serious lightheartedness either going on or coming in for the client. This is true regardless of whether the reading is focused on relationships, financial ventures, or projects. They all point toward success and celebration. This card indicates a happy, comfortable home with contentment and stability around money and jobs.

Depending on where this card shows up in the reading, the benefits will be coming in soon or are available for the taking right now. Eyes wide open, please! Anyone with muddy thoughts about past losses or heartaches will miss this valuable and benevolent opportunity to celebrate a decent dose of good fortune.

We live on a planet of free choice. Wherever our focus is, our world is. There are opportunities around us all the time. Being preoccupied distracts from the available bounty. This card can stand alone and splash good light on cards around it. In general, this card shows a settled quality on all matters.

It doesn't change if reversed, but some advisors will read it as their clients having a sense of insecurity, even though they have a stable situation. If this is the case, you have a lot to talk about with your client. You can ask what they feel is in their lives that is unsteady, since the card indicates that all is in balance.

The **4 of Wands (a stable foundation)** and the **2 of Cups (collaboration)** and **Hierophant (religious traditions)** in a love reading indicate the relationship is leaning toward a serious commitment, even proposals of marriage. If already engaged, then it indicates a run of luck with your wedding plans.

The **4 of Wands (a stable foundation)** in a love reading is always good news! The person bringing this great card to the table feels there is enough history with their partner to have a level of security. This is also true when reading for work, career, and projects. There is enough solid ground under all situations to succeed.

Reversed 4 of Wands (stable foundation) means someone may be losing faith and trust in a situation even though the foundation is firm. If reading for someone after a breakup who is interested in what their ex is thinking, the reversed 4 will mean they remember the foundation that was built, but their insecurity from the breakup makes them feel there is nothing to come back to or build upon. In this particular case, if there was going to be a reconciliation, it would have to happen after a clean break, where the two can come back completely fresh, usually after a fair amount of time apart.

9
FIVE OF WANDS

(Arguing, Gossip, Frustration)

All 5s will indicate that change is happening now or coming soon. The purpose of discomfort is to shine a light on what isn't working in your life. In most Tarot decks, images of this card depict a defensive stance with Wands pointed at each other, but notice that none are touching. This is the classic low burn of petty gossip and the annoying actions of short-tempered snaps toward friends and loved ones.

The 5 is indeed a relatively low number, but make no mistake: too much of this on a daily basis will erode the happiest person into a sour mood. This card will point to a person's ego coming from hubris due to immaturity, or simple stress overload. How stubborn you are about how you think things *should* be determines whether this 5 is going to be comfortable (being aware of the situation and course correcting) or uncomfortable (snap decisions and assumptions that aren't accurate).

If your client's questions are about work, encourage them to stop participating in all office gossip immediately. Warn that it will be tempting to continue talking or complaining about business to others, but tensions are (or will become) high enough to trip everyone up, and the office dynamic will suffer. If the reading is about love, this tells me that there's been underlying bickering throughout the relationship, most likely due to unspoken expectations that lead to insecurities. Having a conversation with a distraught client who just had a bad fight leading to a breakup is heartbreaking. When I see this 5 in the reading, I know to say, "Stop taking your partner's bait; both of you are triggered by little things, and then both of you grow into frustration. Once you are pulled into the drama, then disappointing and even childish actions start happening. The surrounding cards in the reading will tell you what topics need to be addressed to clearly see the situation.

The 5 of Wands (arguing, frustration) with Pentacles leans into frustration about the tangible "things" in our lives. This is a fear of losing possessions or position in the office or standing in the community. The chances of getting clear and concise questions from your client may not be good, so make sure you notice the suit category so you, as the advisor, can stay centered.

...

5 of Wands is poor actions due to a frustrating situation.

5 of Wands with Cups: poor actions caused by confusing emotions

5 of Wands with Swords: poor action because of overthinking or obsessive thinking about a situation

5 of Wands with Pentacles: poor actions with resources, putting possessions, acquisitions, and health in jeopardy

The 5 of Wands reversed (real harm comes from arguing) means watch out, because the chances are high that no one is going to win. When upright, there is room for understanding. When upright, you can help a client back up far enough to see where someone could have misunderstood their intentions or where they may have gotten confused by a situation. Then, immediately, course-correct. Reversed means a person has held on to their end of the rope way too long, and now there is a high probability of causing real damage in the particular situation.

RULE FOR FIVES

5 of Wands upright is recognizing that a problem is happening, while the reversed is being stubborn with that problem.

5 of Cups upright is feeling guilt and remorse about what happened. Reversed is coming to terms with loss and starting new.

5 of Swords upright signals active disputes, while reversed signals that damage has been done from the conflict and there's not much more to do or say.

5 of Pentacles upright is not using your resources wisely regarding health and money. Needing help but not asking for it.

Reversed (depending on where the card falls in the throw) means you either have the strength to rise above or will achieve success after a period of hardship.

⑩

SIX OF WANDS

(Success and Fulfillment)

No sooner does the 5 of Wands get us off track with petty arguments and corrosive gossip, the 6 of Wands put us right back on. This indicates the worst is over, and people are noticing you with respect and appreciation. For the most part, this card shows a balance of self-confidence and graciousness.

On occasion, if the neighboring cards are challenging or the whole spread is ill dignified, this card can mean hubris and self-centeredness. It represents someone who thinks they are better than everybody else. A layout or spread like that doesn't happen often, but it still does enough for me to feel that it's worth mentioning here.

As a stand-alone card, it is a welcome sight for people who have worked hard on a task or project. Also, as an advisor, I like to mention to the client that others have noticed and are impressed with their work and work ethic. These are folks behind the scenes, and this message, it is hoped, uplifts a client who has put in some diligent work on the topic. So many times, those who appreciate us or admire us don't say anything. For whatever reason, they're quiet about it. As an advisor, I'm happy when the opportunity to share this information shows up.

The **6 of Wands (success and fulfillment)** with the **3 of Pentacles (apprentice / good at work)** means you are being noticed by management or admired by a friend or love interest for accomplishments. Add the **6 of Pentacles (period of generosity)** and you can look forward to a promotion or raise (or both).

The **6 of Wands (success and fulfillment)** with the **8 of Wands (events go fast)** indicates you can look forward to swift advancement.

The **6 of Wands (success and fulfillment)** with some majors such as the **Star (hope)**, **Sun (self-expression)**, or the **World (triumphant success)** shows an enhancement and will magnify the benefits.

The **6 of Wands (success and fulfillment) reversed** but all other cards being positive indicates that your client either lacks self-worth or is so incredibly humble they truly don't see others lauding them.

The **6 of Wands (success and fulfillment)** reversed with negative cards, such as the **Devil (obsessive compulsions)**, will show you narcissism or inflated pride. If the reading is for or about a young child, they will be show-offs striving for approval and recognition. The same can be true for adults but will come across more as overt competitiveness. Either way, it's a person who needs recognition for their efforts to stay feeling good about themselves. The Devil shows us that their ways of getting that recognition will be destructive.

The **6 of Wands (success and fulfillment)** with the **5 of Swords (conflict, indecision)** or **7 of Swords (devious illusion)** says to keep a lookout, because someone gets to the top or gains the spotlight by manipulating others. Through work it may mean someone taking credit for work you did, and in love it will mean you are with someone who doesn't have your best interest in mind. In other words, you will never be right or have the last word on anything.

⑪
My Girlfriend Is Cheating!
The Answer May Surprise

I once had a client sit with me and swear that his girlfriend was cheating. He gave me all the reasons that pointed to her betraying the agreement they'd made to be exclusive. But there wasn't anything he could point to that said she was actually seeing someone else. He kept repeating, I told her, "The only reason I would ever leave you is if you started seeing someone else. And I know she is seeing someone else, but I can't prove it." Of course, some of her behavior has gotten him wondering—so much so that he has decided to sit in front of a psychic for answers. "Are you living together yet?" I asked. He answered, "No, not yet, but now I don't know if I want to take that step."

This was an interesting read as the cards, one by one, hit the table, and the picture became clear. Soon I found out what was really going on in the relationship, and it wasn't anything either of us thought!

I began with the Celtic Cross spread. I encourage all of my students to hold off talking about what each card means as they hit the table, because the whole picture needs all the cards upright at the same time. Sometimes the first several cards will tell me more about my client than the specific question. Some cards will tell me how my client is really feeling and not how he *says* he's feeling. Some cards may tell me how my client processes information. I tell him that this reading will reveal how she sees the situation from her point of view.

For the record, I never tell a client that their partner is cheating, because I believe that psychics can't see if it's a physical or emotional distraction. You can be tapping into their POI (person of interest) right when they're reading a romance novel and the sexual tension is high. She isn't cheating, but the energy that you as an advisor will see will show up like there *is* cheating. Be careful. Imagine the hardship you can cause a relationship if you interpret that high tension as a real-life affair. Here is the reading.

5 of Wands (arguing/gossip) situation position = bickering with him and gossiping about troubles behind him, a wave of low-level anger and resentment his girlfriend can't put into words, and she has started talking to friends about her frustration. Most likely getting all kinds of bad advice. When we complain to our friends about someone we love, our friends always take our side. If you need advice about a love situation, talk to someone who isn't a friend of yours, someone who can take a neutral position.

Knight of Pentacles reversed (feeling insecure)—crossed position = what's challenging/influencing the situation = Pentacles means money and possessions and, in regard to this struggling relationship, means not progressing into a tangible declaration of security, such as moving in together. She may just be tired of waiting for him to move forward. Even though we think Pentacles are material things, relationships fall into this suit because a relationship *is* a material thing. Relationships are about planning, effort, and gifts expressing emotional declaration.

Every healthy relationship progresses. If my client has promised a future with her yet hasn't taken action about moving in together or started conversations about the future, she may just be pretending she's dating others when really she just hopes her actions will provoke him into the next steps. If this is true, it shows an immaturity level no one would find attractive, yet, here we are. The rest of the reading will tell me if I'm on the right track. In regard to moving forward in relationships, people leapfrog each other in readiness to settle in. It's natural for a woman to want positive steps of security outside of just promises. Men can father children at 60 years old; women can't. Men just don't get that part and can be much slower to commitment. Next card.

Magician (manifesting)—below the cross position, what a person is feeling inside. His girlfriend is trying to manifest a progression in the relationship. At this point, I could ask my client how long they have known each other, but it wouldn't matter if it was five months or five years. She is trying to move the train forward. He has declared he wouldn't leave her unless she dated someone else, so I have to assume it's long enough to have had the exclusivity conversation, and her anticipation to be engaged is strong.

Page of Cups reversed (immaturity)—above the cross, what is showing on the outside = all the Tarot books point to pages as being messages about whatever suit they belong to—in this case, love—or they are children who carry traits from that suit—in this case, a very sensitive child. Well, it doesn't mean either in this reading. Remember, I'm looking behind a person's eyes and seeing the world through her perspectives and opinions. The reversed Page of Cups shows immature behavior. He's not imagining her implying there's someone else in her life. But I can tell it's only an act. So far, at least, I don't have anyone else in her life. I don't see another Court card (a Knight that would be a peer or around her same age) with anything else around it to imply there's a real person interested in stealing her away.

High Priestess (intuition)—to the left of the center card, **direct past**. This will tell me what happened in the last month or so to influence the situation. This is a highly spiritual card that encourages patience and to listen to your instincts. The tricky part about this particular combination, the **Magician (manifesting or creating something real)** and the **High Priestess (using your intuition)**, is that no one can hold intuition in their hands. Looks to me as if my client, as wonderfully in love as he may appear, has relaxed his good-boyfriend behavior (being available and attentive) to the point where his girlfriend is feeling insecure about their future together. She has said all she could say and dropped all the hints she can think of to get him to talk about the future with her and hammer down a date.

For those of you who aren't familiar with the Celtic Cross spread, the first five cards show what is going on right now in a person's thoughts/actions, including people (represented by Court cards) as well as influencing events throughout the last month. So far, I see a woman desperate for reassurance that her relationship with the man she loves is still on track for a happily ever after, and not a person interested in dating others. The *next* five cards will tell the most probable future if things remain the same and he keeps questioning her and pulling his love back.

The **10 of Swords (feeling betrayed):** This position speaks of the **direct future**, and I read in one-month increments. So this is what's most likely in store to happen for his girlfriend (remember, I'm reading *her*, not him) in the next 30 days. Up until now, she fears her man is falling out of love with her and her dreams of marriage are fading. This 10 says that things will not improve on their own, and she eventually feels completely betrayed by him. She will begin to feel that the promises he gave her were lies, and she is devastated. She will be blaming him and not accepting any of her own behavior as an influence for this outcome. Her poor choices are a *come and get me, come and fight for me* behavior that will surely backfire. Rarely does the pushing away from the one you love to see if he pursues you again work.

The **7 of Wands (defending position)**—in the area of **how she feels about herself** = she is feeling self-righteous about teasing him about other men in her life because it's all about defending her position. He's not treating her the way she feels he should, so she will be defensive about her availability. I realize her actions may seem hard to follow, but remember the reverse page we saw earlier in the reading? And the 5 of Wands as the first card? Instead of acting like an adult, being brave, and using her adult words to discuss her insecurities with the man she loves, she chooses to act out her insecurity by pushing him away and testing his love. It's manipulating, not to mention chaotic, and one of the quickest ways to ruin a good relationship.

The **8 of Wands (fast-moving energy)**: This position speaks of **her environment**, not just home but work as well. Because this 8 has everything to do with moving forward, it symbolizes to me that her heart and mind want to progress in her life and not have things stay the same. My best guess at this point in the reading is that she's involved with friends and coworkers who are getting married, and she has been invited to baby showers and bridesmaid events—and is beginning to feel left behind.

The **9 of Swords (worry)**: This is the **hopes and fears** position in the spread. Our girl is all in her head about this and is losing sleep.

The **3 of Wands reversed (distance between)**—**outcome position**. The 10th card in the lineup explains it all. Through the eyes of my client's girlfriend, she feels a distance, and with all the Swords (thoughts) and Wands (actions) in the reading, she is a jumble of anxiety. She feels her man and relationship slipping away because of not being able to identify and put words to why she is feeling sad, lost, and alone. She feels she can't show her hand and doesn't feel safe being truthful for fear that he isn't ready and will ask her to wait longer.

My reading as presented to my client:

"Looking behind your girlfriend's eyes, it's clear she isn't seeing anyone else." He sits up straighter in his chair and declares once again, "I know she's cheating; I know it!" I wait until he settles in again, then say, "You made her a promise that the only time you would step back from the relationship is if she was cheating. I see you may have overpromised." He looks puzzled and asks why. I continue: "I sense you've had second thoughts about marrying your girlfriend for a little while, because you have pulled away a bit. While nothing was said out loud, her sensitivities picked up your hesitation. Neither one of you talked about this shift because neither has the words to explain it, so you both just went into your perceived modes: you pulling away a bit because you have become uncertain about her as a partner, and her feeling the distance and acting out so you pay attention to her. Then you, surprised at her poor behavior on the inside, yet trying to pretend she is the one for you on the outside, have complicated things. Relationships have difficult spots, and I'm happy you are trying to understand the situation. The bottom line is she is afraid she is losing you. Both of you are really intuitive with each other. The struggle for both is real.

"It's normal to go in and out of devotion after committing to another. Mainly because we all take on new personas and personalities with every new definition in the relationship. The expectations we have for each other inside a casual boyfriend-girlfriend status are much different than the expectations of being exclusive and commitment toward marriage. When you declare that you were devoted to the relationship and happily ever after, she didn't perceive your actions change from boyfriend status to exclusive status. It's an unspoken thing, but real as can be. Words and actions don't meet. She wanted to start talking and planning that future, house, kids, wedding; but, as best as I can tell, you didn't open or initiate those topics. Am I correct?"

He nodded. "Yes," he said. "It felt like things were going too fast."

I continued: "First, let me say that you can leave a person for any reason, and I think it was awesome you made that declaration to her when you became exclusive. You know now that there are so many other reasons to leave someone other than infidelity. You know that now, don't you?"

He nodded.

"So, let me clear things up, and you can decide what to do afterward. Your girlfriend is not seeing anyone. She *is* doubting your word, though. As mentioned earlier, you declared a level of devotion with your words in a heartfelt way. At that moment, her energy shifted, and she handed over her entire heart, and she no longer had eyes for anyone else. You felt the weight of that responsibility and got a little distant and carried on in boyfriend mode and didn't up-level to future-husband mode. You may not have even realized it. You went on with life like normal when, for your girlfriend, life was certainly not normal. Not at all. She was visualizing activities, such as wedding plans and where you would live, and your energy stopped with the words. She metaphorically surrendered her heart, and as the days and weeks ticked by, without planning that future her pain and confusion got worse. So her actions today are to test your words, test your love, test the level of trust you have for her. I haven't read your cards, only hers, but the answer is clear. She only has eyes for you, but because the conversations are not about the future together, she feels you've already left her. This deep despair has triggered some unusual and even inappropriate behavior of hot and cold, push and pull. You're not fond of the woman she has become under all this anxiety. She's not able to find her words and has decided to just act out. Yes, it's immature, but this is who she is. If you don't like the person she is under duress, then say something, negotiate in the name of the woman you fell in love with. Ideally, once the conversation is started, an understanding can be reached. To be a man of your word, you need to really think about the words. Because it is human nature to test a person's word. She loves you deeply and is testing those words by being obnoxious, stubborn, and contradictory. But she is being faithful. This is a cry for attention and understanding. It is the wrong way to ask for it, granted, but she doesn't have the words or, apparently, good counsel."

My client better understood the situation and decided to take her out to talk. He now knows what his words meant to her. I wondered if he would adjust and lean into a progressive relationship or get cold feet and leave her. I walked him to the door, and when I went back into my reading room, I shuffled the cards with that very question in mind. I threw one card, faceup. Judgment. Ah, resurrection. They will rise above this. They will take all the effort and goodwill they have already put toward a healthy relationship and stand firm on it while sorting this little rough patch out.

⑫
SEVEN OF WANDS

(Defending Your Position)

The message of this card is simple: it's time to stand your ground. Either your client will have an impulse already to stand firm on a topic, or your reading will provide the needed confidence to be able to hold firm on a topic. This is a card of courage as well. That being said, it has been my experience that this card is a little different for money than for love. For work or business, it is a clear message to hold your ground, your price, your theory on whatever you're doing. This would also say to hold on to and not move forward in a situation. If the question is to buy or sell something, the 7 of Wands says, "No; hold your ground, stay put," for the time being. The message for money feels too strong of a card in a love reading, however-er. I've noticed through all the readings I have done regarding love that this one will stall communication. It holds way too much anger and boldness for a healthy relationship. I get a hint of immaturity if it comes up in a small squabble and points to a much deeper problem than whatever the topic was that caused the trouble.

On the other hand, if you are advising about a divorce or court dates, it's a business point of view that's best. If it is a love relationship that has hit a bit of a rocky patch, inform with kindness that either your client or their POI is being a bit stubborn in their declarations. Things usually shift in a few days, but the presence of this card today gives you the heads-up that this person doesn't have the capability, at the moment, to negotiate maturely.

The **7 of Wands (defending position) reversed** shows that a person is confused and can't figure out how to handle a problem. That would also indicate someone yielding to another person's opinion or way of doing things. Reversed is not a bad thing at all. It shows you're flexible. The way you are framing the question or problem will lead you to a sound answer.

The **7 of Wands (defending position)** plus the **Justice (contracts)** or **Emperor (corporations)** and most all **Pentacles** (tangible items such as money and property) indicates that wherever the negotiations are at the time of the reading, Spirit is saying hold your ground and don't move forward. Even if you are up against authority.

The **7 of Wands (defending position)** and the **Ace of Swords (rising above adversity)** *after* the 7 show a situation worth fighting for that's likely to succeed.

The **7 of Wands (defending position)** plus the **2 of Swords (stalemate)** shows it won't matter how much you try; there will not be a change in the situation.

The **7 of Wands (defending position)** close to the **5 of Wands (group conflict)** (or any other 5, for that matter). You may be getting set up to fight another person's battle or being drawn in to speak about opposing sides. Either way, this is a delicate combination. Most often, the client won't get far with their efforts.

The **7 of Wands (defending position)** and the **5 of Cups (guilt and remorse)**. Well, you can tell with these two that your client may regret fighting the current battle. Is this the mountain to die on? This combination says no!

The **7 of Wands (defending position)** and **Temperance (stay balanced with diplomacy)**. Temperance is telling you *how* you defend your position. It doesn't mean you give up and agree, but compromise on some level may be in your best interest.

⓭
EIGHT OF WANDS

(Fast-Moving Energy)

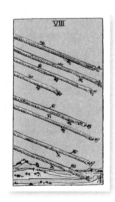

This card represents going in a straight line with speed and lighthearted freedom. The **8 of Wands** points to **spontaneous action** without thought. This card shows the energy of the asked-about topic moving so fast that it can indicate air travel. If this card is teamed up with another that points to family—**6 of Cups (family and old friends)**, **4 of Wands (stable situation)**, **10 of Pentacles (legacy)**, and/or **Judgment (resurrecting the past)**, Spirit is saying my client may be traveling to a family reunion.

I mention these little tidbits because some combinations are so reliable so much of the time that I tell a client about it (even if it is off topic). If it doesn't ring true for the moment, I suggest they put the information in their pocket and it will come to mind when plans start going out. Nine times out of ten, that family reunion invitation shows up soon after the reading. This reading type comes up again with different cards later in the book.

In a love reading, it can indicate fast-moving feelings, so fast that the feelings of love may be unsustainable. It can indicate love that burns hot and burns out within a few weeks. To have that be the message, there will need to be supporting cards pointing to that scenario. Those cards would be the **Ace of Cups (new love)**, **Lovers (physical passion)**, **Page of Cups (young love, loving with abandon)**, and/ or **the Chariot (focus on one direction)**. It may be going so fast that control of the situation can't be achieved. Don't think that the presence of this card in a love reading means that passions burn out—no, not at all. It appears to shine the light, however, that it may be time to energetically slow down and become more relaxed and less intensely focused on one person. But the ride into crazy love is so fun, right? Enjoy. Keep one hand on the wheel and seat belts fastened at all times.

A reading focusing on a job or work situation says you can make quick, split-second decisions proving rapid gains. Events are always fast around the Wands, but the number 8 pours jet fuel on it (in a good way), and your talents shine right through the blaze. As mentioned earlier, sometimes it is indicative of air travel, so if the topic is career, money, business, or job related, there may be options to create profits during travel.

The **8 of Wands (fast-moving energy)** with **2 of Swords (stalemate)** can be a deadlock that stalls momentum quickly. But you have ways around this 2. Think, think. New ideas are your secret weapon.

The **8 of Wands (fast energy)** showing up *after* the **7 of Wands (holding your position)** shows blasting through a stubborn situation.

The **8 of Wands (fast energy)** *after* **3 of Swords (heartbreak)** shows a quick recovery.

The **8 of Wands (fast-moving energy) reversed** slows, stalls, or even cancels negotiations. You won't have ways around this slowdown. I see this a lot in love readings after the couple has an argument. It just shows that the person I'm reading for needs a break from the conflict. To have this card indicate a complete break in the relationship, there should be more cards pointing to that, such as the **Death** card (**natural ending**) or **reversed Justice (broken agreements and contracts)**.

The **8 of Wands (fast energy)** and the **reversed Chariot** point to the same conclusions of stopping progress. The Chariot also indicates road travel. Don't drive fast and furious when the above combination shows up. Could mean that speeding offers grave consequences. Other cards in the spread will add their messages, bringing about a full story with action steps.

NINE OF WANDS

(Don't Give Up)

Don't give up—success is right around the corner is the message for this particular 9.

This card tells the advisor to be extra kind to whomever this belongs to, the client or the client's POI. This person is so overwhelmed with life that they are ready to give up. If you're reading for yourself, it is Spirit recognizing that you are doing well, and they are with you. This is definitely a card of encouragement. The message of success being "right around the corner" will be welcome news, even though people may not believe you at the moment. Spirit is recognizing a person's hard work and the effort they have already spent on this work project or love relationship. Tell them the momentum they have established will keep building positively, and they can relax while still moving forward. There are forces behind the scenes working on your behalf.

The **9 of Wands (hang in there)** shows there isn't a lot of emotional currency left in this person. If you are reading about someone of interest (their POI) for your client, caution against any deep or deliberating conversations with their person right now. It will be too big of a conversation and may jeopardize the relationship altogether because their person is simply exhausted by circumstances.

There are times when the **9 of Wands (don't give up)** should be considered a huge stop sign, however. This 9 tells you that the person this was thrown for won't be able to serve clients' needs because they are way too overwhelmed by the situation. In a love reading, it doesn't matter how badly you want to talk things out with your partner; being quiet and supportive is what your person needs right now.

This 9, for the most part, is to shout encouragement to the person it belongs to, but here are a few combinations when you encourage a person to let go. The following combinations will make this clear.

If the **9 of Wands (feeling overwhelmed and ready to give up)** is followed by any of these cards, the combination will most likely have these trajectories. These examples give you enough information to have your client entertain the thought that giving up is indeed the best thing to do, since the outcome isn't going to be worth the effort. The first is the **reversed 9 of Wands (cut your losses)**.

The **9 of Wands (overwhelmed)** and **4 of Cups (indifference)**. The situation may not be worth working out, since all the work in the relationship or work project is falling flat, and there is no motivation to create success by others. No teamwork.

The **9 of Wands (overwhelmed)** and **10 of Swords (failed plans and defeated)**. Don't bother fighting through the exhaustion, since success may not be available in the end.

The 9 of Wands encourages you to persevere, however. If it is coupled with the **10 of Wands (overwhelmed and uneven burdens)**, it looks like you are fighting to keep doing more for others. This is a very unbalanced situation. Sometimes I find this combination when there is one person in a relationship who is having a health crisis, and the responsibilities to keep the family going fall to their partner. This is the combination that prompts you to suggest respite care services.

Staying with this same combination, if you have a **reversed Court card** (any suit)—for example, any of the Pages (Pages in Court cards represent children), you can mention that you see a child or dependent person who is causing some overwhelmingness. If perhaps you have a reversed King or Queen (indicating an elder) mentioned, you see a dependent parent or adult. Reversed Court cards may point to people involved who are causing blocks and restrictions. On a positive note, any of the **successful cards that follow this 9** mean that success is on the horizon, if cards such as the **Ace of Swords (rising above adversity)**, the **Sun card (freedom to self-express)**, or the **World (successful ending, feeling triumphant)** are close by.

If an ace of any suit is present around a challenging card, such as the 9 of Wands, it will lighten and brighten the situation.

⑮
TEN OF WANDS

(Uneven Burdens)

This card highlights a person taking on the burdens of another, and the situation is exhausting for them. Your client's responsibilities are weighing heavily on them. Some examples of the 10 of Wands in daily life would be doing the lion's share of the work with children, elderly, or disabled adults—all represented by any of the Pages in the deck. I sometimes see this 10 when the responsibilities of the partnership or marriage are uneven due to one person having an illness or employment challenge, much like the **9 of Wands (don't give up)**; however, the 9 of Wands shows a successful horizon, whereas the 10 will need the cards around it to tell you if a path to success is available. This 10 tells you that spirit sees your hard work and is sending help. This is a good time to look at how much is on your plate and how much of the obligation you are feeling is real, assumed, or expected. It's been my experience that our lives can get overwhelming because we say yes to things when we need to say no. People who are empaths will find themselves with this 10 in their readings. They are excellent at anticipating another person's needs or mistakenly assume that life will be too hard on that other person if they don't help, so they feel compelled to step in. We all will have opportunities to work hard and for longer hours on another's behalf. It can be very satisfying knowing you lightened the burden of another. Quite simply, life will hand you moments where Spirit asks you to work a bit harder for the benefit of someone else. And it feels right to give. Parents may need help either physically or financially. Children hit a rough spot and require schedules changed or specific situations focused on. You pick up the loose ends at work to show management you have a sense of ownership and pride. A partner may be sidelined because of a complicated and challenging illness or situation where you need to temporarily provide for them. A word of caution, however, with advisors seeing this card surrounded by cards that point to a cry for attention: the **reversed 6 of Wands (you still have work to do before you can call yourself a success)** comes to mind. In a love reading, the **6 of Wands (pride and a desire to. be noticed)** is a perfect example of this 10 working the shadow side of the situation. Regarding business, the **10 of Wands (uneven burden)** with the **6 of Wands (being noticed by others)** and the **10 of Swords (betrayal)** means there may be a project that will take a lot of effort, and people may leave you to take the entire task on. Will this be worth that time and effort? The advice should encourage your client to read the fine print on a project before saying yes. If they do not, people may just leave them with the whole thing. Of course, informing your client that this scenario is syncing up gives them an opportunity to stand their ground and make sure that tasks others are to provide are written down. Knowing a situation will turn like this doesn't mean you need to run in the other direction. It's life giving you chance to shine with brilliance and boldness.

If the **Devil (obsessions)** is close to this **10 (overburdened)**, you may be obsessing over an outcome and taking on too much because of *your own* control issues.

In a love reading, watch for the signs that you are doing all the heavy lifting in the relationship, only to get an "Oh, thanks" in the end. It's like doing things just for social media "likes." The substance isn't there, and that can lead to a feeling of being taken advantage of.

For business, **10 of Wands (uneven burden)** and **Justice (legal contracts)** together suggest that one should read the small print in all written correspondences—contracts, emails, or texts—because you may not fully understand what you're getting into.

The **10 of Wands (uneven burden)** and the **3 of Pentacles (fine worker)** can indicate management overworking you because you are awesome in your job. Similarly, these could mean a promotion with a lot more responsibilities coming their way.

The **10 of Wands (uneven burden)** and the **Devil (obsessive-compulsive)** may boil down to a workaholic.

If perhaps you have the **10 of Wands (uneven burden)** and a love card such as the **Ace of Cups (new romance or collaboration)** or the **2 of Cups (purposeful partnership)**, or both, it may indicate that while life is already a big burden for you, there is the excitement of a new project or person, and your schedule may get bumpy while you try to fit everything in.

The **10 of Wands (uneven burden)** *followed by the* **9 of Wands (ready to give up)** means you have taken on more than you think you can handle but will most likely succeed. What would the message be if these cards were flipped? If you have the **9 of Wands (ready to give up)** *followed by the* **10 of Wands (uneven burden)**, just as before, you have taken on more than you think you can handle, and success is not as sure. The 9 says you can't take on any more without your life going out of balance. Throwing more obligations or expectations at this person may break a relationship, job, even career goals.

Did you notice that the pattern in the story changed just by taking the same two cards and putting them in a different order? A favorable card after this 10 will bring a positive outcome for your efforts.

Blocks and restrictions with reversed Court cards or unfavorable cards after this 10, most likely, will not have a good outcome. This information can help a person make a clear-eyed decision from this point and decide to continue to serve or leave this unbalanced commitment.

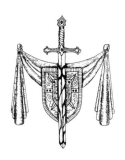

⑯
ACE OF SWORDS

(*Rising above Adversity*)

ACE of SWORDS.

Since all Aces mean "new beginnings" and the suit of Swords has everything to do with the mind, thoughts, and communication, the Ace of Swords means a new and fresh idea.

Where it lands on your table will tell you if this brilliant idea is here now or will arrive soon. Either way, something wonderful is happening! Aces are always good news, and this one, in particular, helps you think quickly and maneuver successfully in all kinds of adversity.

As you will notice in this combination section, when any of the Wand suit sits close to this ace, you can be sure you have not only clear ideas but enough momentum to bring those new ideas into action.

Ace of Swords (clear thoughts) with any **Wand (action)** means your client most likely already knows what direction to move in, and you as the advisor can help define clear steps to take. Trust yourself because you are being guided well.

Ace of Swords (clear thoughts) at the end of a throw is a welcome sight because it shows that whatever the adversity you are going through now or before this ace, it won't be bringing you down.

Ace of Swords (clear thoughts) *after* the **2 of Swords (stalemate)** means successful negotiations or a breakthrough from a deadlock situation in relationships.

Ace of Swords (clear thoughts) after **Justice (legal matter / contracts)** or **Lovers (collaborations)** means a favorable ending.

Ace of Swords reversed (unclear thinking) means an idea isn't viable to move forward, or Spirit is saying you should set that idea aside for now. This could also indicate a delay or breakdown in communications.

Ace of Swords reversed is saying you are not communicating well enough for the other people involved to favor your position. Are you talking over everyone's head? If talking about someone's job, tell them that this combination suggests that their customers may not really understand the offer being sold to them. Regarding love, are you making it clear to your husband or wife what your position or viewpoint is? Not likely. You may feel clear as rain, but Spirit is saying there are miscommunications going on.

The **Ace of Swords reversed** could be saying that your client isn't communicating at all and is just assuming their partner automatically understands what they're thinking. After all, they know you've been under pressure. They know you've put in a lot of overtime, right? Why are they mad? You assume they knew, but this card is saying they don't understand. In fact, your partner may start harboring some hard feelings about it. Forewarned is forearmed, as they say. Best to use your words. Don't assume that others understand.

TWO OF SWORDS

(Stalemate)

Swords are all about thinking things over, then thinking them all over again.

This 2 means that decisions may take awhile and are slowing or possibly coming to a complete stop. The message is to take a break or a long pause regarding the question at hand.

If I have a love question such as "My boyfriend and I fought last night; how is he feeling about the situation today?," the answer is clear. He is not moving forward with any communication right now. It doesn't mean the relationship is over; however, this 2 describes your client's most advantageous next steps: meaning not to pester, prod, or force conversation right now. As much as a partner may want to resolve the issue right now . . . right now is not the time.

It will depend on where this 2 is placed in the reading, but it has been my experience that wherever it lands, it slows everything down around it. So for love, it means taking a break and letting things sit. As uncomfortable as that may sound, it would be best, in the long run, to let a few days pass before talking about things.

In regard to money, this is the time to have quiet faith in your ideas and wisdom. Things slow down, but you have clear thinking and ideas on your side. Whatever your communication was before this 2 came into the reading, feel confident that you've said enough of all the right things.

The **2 of Swords (stalemate)** *after* the **2 of Cups (relationship)** with the **3 of Swords (heartbreak)**: whatever was said or done has affected the person of interest deeply and will need time to heal, then a reassessment of the relationship, project, or investment will, most likely, be next steps.

The **2 of Swords (stalemate)** with **5 of Wands (quarrels)** or the **5 of Swords (conflict)** means that momentum forward stops or should stop because, if you keep pushing the issue, your partner (or work project) will leave—maybe for good.

The **2 of Swords (stalemate)** with the **Hermit (quiet thinking)** means don't press the situation. Instead, allow the other person to be alone with their thoughts. They are assessing the situation through a spiritual heart.

The **2 of Swords (stalemate)** with **Temperance (diplomacy)**. The 2 is telling you there is a stalemate, and the Temperance card is saying to negotiate with discretion and sensitivity in the situation.

The **2 of Swords (stalemate)** with the **Tower (destruction of the old)**. Tower brings change from the outside of your situation, which means that during this pause, a major restructuring is taking place. In love, this combination indicates that the person has been crushed by an event or harsh words, a situation outside their control, and this pause is necessary for them to decide if the situation, project, or relationship is worth rebuilding. In business, this combination tells you that the break will cause many shifts in the workforce or titles, and possibly your involvement in the project may be phased out. Not to worry though. These uncomfortable earthquakes usually settle out in your favor. Everything is rebuilt better.

The **2 of Swords (stalemate)** and **Devil (obsessive/compulsive actions)** in a love reading mean that the pause or break in the relationship is bringing out the worst in a person. I find this combination when there is possible stalking. In a reading on your own business, this combination indicates hard feelings about the negotiations. Someone may have an impulse to sabotage the situation. Could it be your client? The owner of the business you are reading about? Many business owners may ask about a certain account that they are responsible for. Not asking about their own business, but one that they manage. The **2 of Swords (stalemate)** may ask you to pause this account because the initial agreement may not be managed well. The Devil will indicate how their workforce is dealing with the situation, possibly with some anger or resentment toward your client. In a love reading, the 2 is telling you to press pause or take a break because either you or your partner is having an unhealthy response regarding the situation at hand. If you get this card combination and you haven't heard from your partner for a while, the Devil is telling you they are distracted by an unhealthy compulsion. That unhealthy compulsion could possibly, but certainly not exclusively be drugs, alcohol, or unhealthy levels of work, sports, or erotica. Either way, don't poke the beast. Let things calm down.

The **2 of Swords (stalemate) reversed** is intriguing because, in my experience, it doesn't mean the opposite of the upright. The reversed 2 doesn't mean that things move forward. It means there is a real imbalance, lots of confusion, or conflict. The upright 2 shows a woman with a blindfold (faith and fairness), and the two swords crossed are the symbols for the pause or slow movement forward on a project. The key to the reversed is faith. People will be duplicitous, two faced, or double dealing. Things remain slow, but the slowness or pause will reveal how people handle this time of intermission. If the 2 of Swords is reversed, pay attention to everyone concerned, since their actions or reactions may have you rethinking the whole situation.

⓲
THREE OF SWORDS

(Grief, Sorrow)

This impressive image shows broken hearts due to quarreling: sharp words, spoken or implied, because of a disappointment or letdown that deeply changes opinions and viewpoints. In my professional life, this heartbreak card suggests unspoken yet unmet expectations one person has about the relationship. This event may shift the focus on how you relate to each other in the future. Even though this 3 is shocking and can set a situation back or stop forward motion in its tracks for a time, I remind clients that this card has the energy of only a 3.

Every card has power and its own place and purpose, but a low number such as a 3, even with a challenging situation like this, means the relationship, project, or business has a good chance of surviving.

When you see the **3 of Swords (disappointment/isolation)**, follow the line of cards backward to see where the hardship or misunderstanding started. Remember the energies of the suits. If Pentacles are close, it most likely signals that misunderstandings or argument are about money or property. Swords? Poor communication. Cups? Mishandling someone's emotions. Wands? Poor judgment regarding an action.

Sometimes distressing situations erupt out of the blue. With the Tarot, you can pinpoint where the two of them, or the group (if the reading is about a job), separated energetic ways. A clear path out of the confusion will be seen clearly through the cards. Simply trace back from this card to see the root of the argument.

The **3 of Swords (heartbreak, grief)** with the **5 of Cups (guilt and remorse)** means regardless of what caused the disruption, that person is feeling really bad about what they said or did. This combination looks as if there will be healing ahead. I measure a person's depth of devotion and commitment in a love reading by the presence of this particular 5 (emotions). People who don't genuinely care don't show guilt or remorse after difficult times of conflict. The presence of the 5 of Cups tells me the person cares but doesn't have the words they need to solve the problem right now.

If this 3 is standing alone in a sea of mundane or even happy cards, the relationship, situation, or frenzied issue should resolve quickly and satisfactorily. However, if coupled with any ill-fated cards, including the ones discussed in the following, here are the most probable outcomes:

The **3 of Swords (heartbreak/quarrels)** followed by the **10 of Swords (disappointment/betrayal) or Moon reversed (hidden agenda)** or **reversed Magician (manipulation)** reveals either that reconciliation isn't available or you shouldn't consider going back at this time, since the motivations and objectives are unclear. Throw in the **Devil (obsessive/compulsive)** and it could even be dangerous.

The **3 of Swords (quarrels, heartbreak)** with the **Hanging Man (pause to rethink)** or **2 of Swords (stalemate)**. This situation calls for a separation, a complete break, if there is going to be a chance to heal.

Look for the **Judgment (resurrection)** card to see if there will be a coming back around soon.

The **3 of Swords (quarrels, heartbreak)** with the **Hermit (going within for spiritual, moral insight)** says a person needs space to think things through alone.

Never go chasing someone whose reading shows the **Hermit (quiet seeker)** card. If they do let you into their life, you won't have their full attention. In fact, your presence or demand for attention may cause resentments. Quiet resentments because of the Hermit. I know that staying quiet when you want to talk it over is harder to do than say, but if you have discipline over your emotions and let time pass, the chance the relationship or friendship survives the conflict increases greatly.

The **3 of Swords (quarrels, heartbreak)** followed by **Temperance (moderation)** shows that Spirit is suggesting you stay centered and balanced for success when dealing with this situation. You will need to yield to the other person's concerns, since Temperance is all about moderation and acceptance.

The **3 of Swords** (**quarrels, heartbreak**) with the **10 of Pentacles** (**family legacy**) or the **6 of Cups** (**old relationships, family of origin**), or both, shows hard feelings and disagreements with family or that an old wound or heartbreak from the past hasn't healed. The conflict will be about money or property, since the **10 of Pentacles** can indicate **inheritance**.

Sometimes in a reading where my client explains that their partner is hesitant to commit to something more permanent, I may see this 3 along with some past cards, such as the ones prior indicating he or she hasn't fully recovered from a past hurt. Also can indicate that the challenging situation happening now is reminding them of past trauma. It's important we don't bring past poor behavior into a current situation. We grow and change. If you are experiencing hardships with a new person, don't hold them up to scrutiny against the last person. No one deserves that.

The **3 of Swords reversed** is a bit better, in general, since it can indicate hurt feelings or disappointment that is kept hidden or that the person is making a bigger deal out of the situation. Advice? Reflect on the cards prior to this 3 to understand the root cause of the disappointment. Once in the light, solutions are quick and lasting. The 3 of Swords is painful but won't last if you are willing to look at a problem, address it, and course-correct with better choices.

⓳
FOUR OF SWORDS

(Rest and Recuperation)

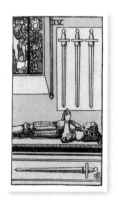

You've been through a lot, and the 4 of Swords says it's time for a rest.

I love this card when it comes up because I get to tell my clients that they can relax; the worst is over. You will probably notice that the image on this card shows four swords close at hand but retired, and the person is lying down. It feels like the angels are saying, "You did such a good job and worked so hard; relax while we look after you." As an advisor, you can acknowledge that your client has worked hard and they require a much-needed time-out for self-care.

If this card comes up in a money reading, this is Spirit telling you that your client is on the edge of burnout and needs the same solution: rest after all that hard work.

Another "pause" card, but here's the difference:

The **2 of Swords (stalemate/pause)** indicates a pause because negotiating has come to an impasse.

The **4 of Swords (rest/pause)** is a choice. Either your client heeds the warning and chooses self-care or suffers the consequences to their emotional or even physical health in the near future.

Some interesting combinations I've come across:

The **4 of Swords (rest/pause)** with the **8 of Swords (feeling restricted—at no choice)**, meaning that the rest or pause is forced upon this person. For good or bad, the card means the same. It would be best for you to take some time away from what has preoccupied you. Add the **Justice Card (courts and contracts)** to this combination, and it shows someone is forced to stop; maybe they are in jail or another kind of state-mandated time-out. A health issue forces you into bed, or a hospital.

The **4 of Swords (rest/pause)** with the **7 of Cups (imagination)** shows you're taking yourself out of the grind to daydream, nap, and create. This 7 has plenty of warning signs on its own, because it indicates an active imagination. The 7 can be problematic because not all of your thoughts are grounded in reality. But the combination with this 4, **taking a pause**, with this 7 equals lots of wonderful ideas and brings in an atmosphere of creativity. Write your novel or screenplay during this time. Carve out a good amount of time to cultivate all the options in your creative brain. This makes for a wonderful way to rest and rejuvenate.

The **4 of Swords (rest/pause)** and the **8 of Pentacles (passionate study)** means taking this time off to study something you really enjoy. Add the **Chariot (road travel)** or **8 of Wands (air travel)**, and this could mean that a desired seminar or workshop away from home is being set up for you.

The **4 of Swords (rest/pause)** with the **Hierophant (traditional religion)** or the **Hermit (quiet seeker / spiritualism and other faith-based topics)**, or both, proposes a retreat, either formal or casual, with spiritualism involved. This could include a time of fasting for religious reasons or a time you set aside to study a sacred methodology.

The **4 of Swords (rest/pause) reversed** usually means a person knows they should rest and risks burnout but continues anyway. We can give so many understandable reasons why we can't take time off to rejuvenate. I've noticed that life has a way of slowing or delaying progress when a person pushes themselves too far. They find themselves unable to manifest in their life because they simply don't have the strength. This next combination will make this 4 clear.

The **4 of Swords (rest)** *upright* means life is pulling up a chair for you to relax in. The **4 of Swords** *reversed* means the chair is still there, but your client is not choosing to sit in it.

❷⓿
FIVE OF SWORDS

(Change/Conflict)

If you haven't caught on by now, the suit of Swords has the most challenging cards holding the most conflict in the deck. The 5 of Swords represents a match of wits and intellect. Sword cards represent headstrong personalities with axes (or swords) to grind. You want to guard against loss and deceit regardless if someone else is causing this disruption or its uneasiness exists inside yourself. It may lead you to cut out important details on projects that really should have your full attention. A person can lose compassion for a loved one when this 5 appears. Be mindful of who is around you and of your own thoughts and impulses for possible gaps in personal integrity. Ideally, you want to see positive cards around this one to make sure all the fuss won't cost you much. Make no mistake: this is a "bull in a china shop" scenario.

The **5 of Swords (change/conflict)** and any of the Kings or Queens will give you an idea of who may be causing the disruption. It's always up to us to decide how to react to something. Knowing who doesn't have your best interest can help sort things out before reacting.

The **5 of Swords (change/conflict)** with the **reversed Magician (manipulator)** or the **Devil (obsessive/compulsive)**, or both, suggests you are in the wrong group of people, to say the least. This is an unhealthy and unsafe situation. Regarding money, business, or career, you need to document everything and remain cautious in all dealings. In a love reading, this situation could get to a place where you think you are losing your mind. This combination shows you are unsafe in the situation or with a person. Dangers such as gaslighting, on the minor side of the spectrum, and violence with a loss, on the other, could be at play.

The **5 of Swords (change/conflict)** with **2 of Swords (stalemate)** means conflict that can't be resolved in its current state. Use the pause of this 2 to remove yourself from the conflict.

If the **Devil (obsession)** is anywhere close, you had best sever all ties quickly.

The **5 of Swords (change/conflict)** or **Page of Swords (delay)**, **7 of Wands (holding position)**, **Hanged Man (pause)**, or a combination of these. Take your break from the situation, with the idea you may not return to negotiate further.

The **5 of Swords (change/conflict)** plus the **8 of Cups (walking away)**. Leaving the situation unexpectedly without consideration to others. Someone is being selfish.

The **5 of Swords (change/conflict)** and the **Moon (Illusions)**: you don't have all the facts, so don't try to sort things out or insist on a resolution right now. In business, do not sign that contract just yet. The reading is telling you that there is something in the paperwork that you don't understand, or (more likely) something has been intentionally hidden from you. Have a second set of eyes to look at your document.

The **5 of Swords (change/conflict)** plus the **5 of Wands (gossip)**. Jealousy from others and possibly slander that could harm your reputation.

If the suit of **Cups (emotion)** is close, the jealousy or slander may be coming from friends or loved ones.

The **5 of Swords (change/conflict)** with the **2 of Wands (creative project)** or **2 of Pentacles (financial partnership)**. You may have a business partner or creative partner who either can't be trusted with your money or won't give you credit for your efforts.

If our **5 of Swords (change/conflict)** comes *after* the **7 of Wands (defending position)**, then it would be clear the defensive person caused the conflict.

If our **5 of Swords (change/conflict)** comes *after* the **5 of Wands (gossip)**, we could be sure gossip is the reason for the conflict.

Let's change it up a little.

The **5 of Swords (change/conflict)** coming *after* the **7 of Swords (potential danger)** would indicate that the conflict will be escalating, and to be careful.

The **5 of Swords (change/conflict)** coming *after* the **6 of Wands (pride, normally a positive card)** could reveal someone jealous. Look for other cards that would show that person moving into action. If the **Devil (obsession)** or **10 of Swords (revenge)** is present, the advisor can build a story with enough detail for the client to be able to successfully navigate the trouble. A client will have a heads-up if she notices petty gossip in the workplace. It is by no means neutral. If your client is the manager, they would want to address it right away. Similarly, if someone in their life was **defending a position (7 of Wands),** they would know that, if pushed, this situation (**5 of Swords, conflict**) may end a friendship.

To sum up this interesting card, it means a swift change in a deceitful or cunning manner. If you have Pentacles close, you need to check on your money and possessions, even if the reading is about love. There is someone somewhere mishandling something tangible, and this person is being secretive about it.

㉑
SIX OF SWORDS

(Smooth Waters)

Right when your anxiety is high with the 5 of Swords, the Tarot moves you into calmer waters. It's like the angels are saying, "Relax; we got you."

The most comforting message is "Be still; all will be well." This reminds us that we don't have to go it alone. When we discover peace, our frequency can hold up and have a positive impact on others if we surrender to it. Look for other cards around this one to get more information about where this rest will come from. If Pentacles, then it will be a rest from the struggles of money, home, or job. If Swords, a respite from overthinking or challenging conversations. If Cups, time for self-care is available; take advantage of it.

In a reading about love and money, the **6 of Swords (smooth waters ahead)** will be welcomed. You'll enjoy cooperation from others and troubling situations improving.

The **6 of Swords (smooth times ahead) reversed** means your client may be unwilling or unable to move away from a troubling situation. Well, you may be thinking, which one is it? Look to the other cards close to this 6 to find the answer. For instance:

The **6 of Swords reversed** with the **7 of Wands (holding your ground)**: your pride may be holding you back from the peaceful waters ahead.

The **6 of Swords reversed** with the **8 of Swords (feeling there is no choice)** means that even though you hate the situation, you don't have enough courage to take a leap of faith and leave it. This is the classic "too good to leave but too bad to stay" scenario. This combination comes up often when someone is financially dependent on an abusive or challenging person.

22
SEVEN OF SWORDS

(Illusion and Tricks)

With the 7 of Swords, we move back into a bit of trouble and potential for danger.

This 7 informs us that a situation needs to be handled with care. Look at the cards just before this one to figure out what area needs special consideration. When this card is coupled with a few other cards—namely, the suit of Pentacles, where money and possessions are involved—it could be a sign of dishonesty or even theft. Check your pockets to make sure your belongings, investments, and holdings are safe. When it shows up in a money reading, it warns *against* moving forward with a deal or project; the risk may be too high. The way you handle this situation is with diplomacy.

If the client is considering a financial investment, this 7 says the risks are too high. Perhaps they haven't been told every detail of the deal. Even worse, they may have been deceived during the presentation.

If this 7 comes up about a job you currently hold, it advises that you don't engage in any kind of confrontation. This card can also shine a light on how your client feels about their job, always needing to work behind the scenes to get things done. It can be exhausting working in a place where you feel you are walking on eggshells. Regarding love, this card asks that you think about why you are with this person. When this card appears in a love reading, the message is to seek compromise and use diplomacy. As an advisor, you will need to use diplomacy to tell the client that the best solution for the moment is not just to "go along to get along." Are they meeting your intellectual and spiritual needs?

I have noticed that the **7 of Swords (illusion/trickery) reversed** is about the same as upright, with one small caveat. There is still the same amount of uncertainty around whom to trust and not being able to see through the fog of a situation. However, with the reversed, some of that illusion is possibly self-induced. Meaning, no one on the outside of your client is pulling the wool over their eyes; it is they imagining the worst. Overthinking the situation can create doubt in all areas. Some true, some not.

As an advisor, consider talking to your client about how they feel about their focused topic (job, money, or their relationship). They may reveal to you that they have been cutting corners on their responsibilities because they are unhappy with the job, financial commitment, or relationship. The main message is to be true to yourself and quit imagining stories about your situation. Wake up and look at what's happening through the lens of facts, not wishes.

If the **Magician (manifestor)** or **Magician reversed (manipulator)** is anywhere around the **7 of Swords (illusion/trickery)**, there is someone in the middle of the mess creating all the chaos. This is especially true if the Magician is reversed. Identify the person and move away from them. Withdraw from all dealings if you can. If you must negotiate, always use discretion and finesse. If you are unable to do that on your own, I suggest hiring someone who can negotiate on your behalf. That is, if the deal is so important you can't walk away.

The **7 of Swords (illusion/trickery)** with the **Emperor (mature man/corporation)** is most likely revealing a boss you need to tiptoe around. Of course, use caution whenever talking with this person. Always respect the hierarchy. This boss will demand that respect, no matter how casual they may appear on the outside. Spirit's message is to use caution when dealing with this person. Always speak to this person with respect, especially if they ask you to be casual with them. It's a trap.

Advisors: if perhaps you have the **7 of Swords (illusion/trickery) reversed** and the **Emperor (corporations) upright** *after*, it might be the client wanting a more casual or friendly relationship with upper management to gain favor. It's up to you to tell them that their strategy won't work. Here is an example of how you can deliver this message: "I can see you work best in a casual setting, but Spirit is suggesting that for at least the next month, you should stop trying to gain favor with lighthearted conversations. The management is looking for business excellence, not team building, right now."

㉓
EIGHT OF SWORDS

(Feeling Helpless / At No Choice)

This card shows a person all wrapped up in their personal assessments of lack and limitations. When you look at the card, it looks as if someone else put those ropes around her and placed her in a jail of daggers; it's her limited thinking that has her feeling trapped. (Remember that Swords are your thoughts. Being trapped in your situation is in your mind.)

Quite often this card will appear when people find themselves in a marriage that is emotionally or financially bankrupt. The situation might be showing that a person is dependent on another for finances, children, or perhaps both. This person believes that circumstances are preventing them from freedom and that they have no choice but to stay in the challenging situation.

It has been my experience that when a person describes the injustices in their lives, and I see this 8 in their reading, Spirit is making it very clear that this person feels they have no choices in the matter, *because to choose differently may take them out of the lifestyle they enjoy.* There are always options! Look to the horizon and see them, then make a plan. Yes, to leave an abusive partner may mean you live in a shelter with your child while you reorganize and unsnarl yourself from your abuser. But this card is saying that your client is willing to risk staying and will try to convince you their choice is justified. This can be a very delicate conversation. My understanding is that people don't see options and are suffering because they choose to stay in an uncomfortable yet familiar situation. Gently guide them to the thought that a person can change their mind at any time without having a reason. A statement like this may help when they, once again, face the harsh reality of their situation.

In the card lineup, I have found that retracing or going back through the cards before this 8 can give you a hint of where the root of the problem started and what area of life it is affecting the most. Then move to the cards after to see what the most probable future will be if everything remains the same. If perhaps a freeing card or triumphant card is in the future, then there isn't a whole lot you need to discuss with your client regarding a strategy to get out of the hardship, since this shows that life will give them the strength to change. The cards after this 8 will reveal the thought patterns and impulses of the person you're reading for, and will show you exactly what is needed to change in their life to rise above this challenge.

Reversed 8 of Swords shows what once felt tight and restrictive is now starting to feel relaxed and freer.

Lots of different combinations can tell you what the specific confinement is. For example:

The **8 of Swords (feeling trapped/helpless)** and **Justice (legal system)** or **King of Swords (man in uniform/government official)**, or both, may indicate prison or home restriction by a court. Same as the **King of Swords (mean-spirited man) reversed** means a dominating man with violent tendency has you feeling at no choice.

The **8 of Swords (feeling trapped/helpless)** with the **10 of Pentacles (family/inheritance)** indicates feeling trapped by a sense of duty to the family of origin.

The same holds true with the **6 of Cups (people and relationships from long-ago past)**. There would be a sense of obligation with a good friend or family member.

The **8 of Swords (feeling trapped/helpless)** with the **Devil (obsessive/compulsive)** may have you feeling trapped in addiction or uncontrollable, impulsive behavior.

Any of the following cards can leave a person feeling trapped in a relationship:

The **8 of Swords (helpless)** with the **Hierophant (traditional religion)** is usually a marriage or an exclusive agreement with one person. This can reflect the sense of obligation with the family of origin, as well as expected devotion to one religion and customs.

The **8 of Swords (feeling helpless)** and the **2 of Cups (close relationship)** means feeling trapped by unspoken expectations with another.

Combinations that can signal a pulling away from feeling trapped are the following:

The **Fool (unexpected blessings)** means that an opportunity to leave the situation will present itself out of the blue, and you need to grab it fast to succeed.

The **Magician (manifestor)** is Spirit reminding you that you have all the things you need to gather resources to succeed.

The **Hanging Man (looking at things from a different perspective)** indicates a rush of inspiration and that a list of new options will be revealed to you.

Strength (grace under pressure) gives you the faith to keep moving toward a solution.

Sometimes this 8 is simply saying, "I am afraid of change," in which case you, as a talented advisor, can be of incredible support with your ability to help navigate the future for your client.

NINE OF SWORDS

(Consumed with Worry)

This card shows that a lot of worrying is going on, and can even indicate sleepless nights for your client.

Make sure to ask how your client has been sleeping. Spirit uses this card to remind people that they are watching and care about their health, both physically and mentally. The suit of Swords has everything to do with our thinking, and this card tells us that you or whoever you are reading for is over-thinking a topic or project and might even be blowing it out of proportion. Worry will throw darts of doubt or fear your way, with a little hook at the end of it. If that hook is set just right, it can keep you up for days wondering, "What if?"

When this 9 shows up, you should acknowledge the mental (Sword) struggle your client is under. Then gently remind them that no one has ever crossed a bridge before coming to it. The right words will come at the right time to the right people. You don't have to rehearse it.

...

While this 9 of Swords points to your client being anxious about something, the surrounding cards will show the cause.

Pentacles would be anxious over possessions or money, maybe job security.

Cups reveal feeling anxious over a love relationship or worried about the welfare of a loved one or pet.

Wands show being nervous about an action you will need to take or should be taking.

Swords is all about overthinking, and you are anxious for anxiety's sake.

...

If a person invites the **9 of Swords (worry)** in for too long, you can be sure they will begin to feel rejected, lonely, and undervalued, because that's what excessive worry does. It wears a person down until they don't recognize themselves and feel very lost.

It's been my experience that the **reversed 9 of Swords** is about the **same** as the upright. Some read it as recovering from overthinking, but I haven't found that to be true. Once this 9 is in the reading, it tends to follow the client around and haunt them into retreating into a negative thought loop. However, once identified and recognized, it can dissipate quickly.

TEN OF SWORDS

(Feeling Betrayed)

Feel like you've been thrown under the bus or otherwise betrayed? People who pull the 10 of Swords may feel under the gun for no reason. Or they have a suspicion that someone has it out for them and may be setting them up to fail. If I'm asked how a coworker feels about my client and the 10 of Swords shows up, I most often say that the person in question should not be considered a friend. There's competitiveness there that they aren't being honest about. Of course, one card does not make an entire reading. There should be a few other cards to support a statement like that, but this 10 can stand on its own, and to dismiss it would be a mistake. Those other cards would be the **7 of Wands (defensive)**, the **6 of Wands (pride/ego)**, the **Devil (obsessive)**, and the **5 or 7 of Swords (not handling a situation properly or a duplicitous person, respectively)**. If this 10 comes after a project or an event, it can indicate a less than positive outcome. The rest of the card lineup will tell you specifics about why.

One time a client said she had just left an interview for a job she really wanted, and she asked me to look into how her performance and résumé were received. I saw she would, most likely, be offered the job, but the **10 of Swords (betrayal)** was near the end of the lineup. I looked at the cards before it and saw the **5 of Wands (gossip)** and the **7 of Swords (illusion)**. I told her the good news about being offered the job but to read the contract thoroughly, since I thought that something previously agreed upon during the interview might have been left out of the final draft. Also (with the 7 of Swords present), I cautioned her to keep a low profile once hired, since not everyone she would be working with had her best interest in mind. Months later, she confirmed that she did get the job and did need to modify the final contract to include promises discussed during the interview but that didn't make it into writing. Going against her normal lighthearted and friendly personality, she kept quiet and professional—not sharing anything personal with anyone until she really got to know people better. It certainly paid off for her. She is making great money, and the troublemakers around the office don't try to involve her in any drama. It isn't an ideal place to work, but a necessary step in her career plan, and she is acing it!

In general, the **10 of Swords** showing **at the end** of a throw indicates a less than positive outcome, but everything is negotiable. It's just a heads-up. You can walk away or consider playing by an educated set of personal rules to keep yourself safe. Remember, just because the cards predict a poor or less than positive outcome doesn't mean you shouldn't continue. Those predictions are assuming you play the game as you normally would. If you are willing to entertain the thought of being a bit more creatively introspective and deliberative, then no one has anything to play against you. With that, you'll always come out ahead. Having an Ace in close range of this 10 shows that the project, action, or investment, may be short lived. Switch off your attachment to the outcome and consider other options.

The **10 of Swords (betrayal/loss)** with the **5 of Pentacles (overspending)** cautions that you may lose your financial footing if the same path is continued. If the **9 of Pentacles (financial comfort)** is close, your feeling of loss may be substantial.

The **10 of Swords (betrayal)** with the reversed **7 of Pentacles (financial savings)** says to pay close attention because you may be losing more than your pocket change.

The **10 of Swords (feeling betrayed)** with the **3 of Pentacles (skill/rewards)** suggests someone may be trying to take credit for your work. Document if you feel someone is going behind your back with projects at work, or if a friend is sabotaging your relationship.

The **10 of Swords (betrayal/loss)** reversed in business means you may be throwing good money after bad.

If the reading is about love, and they are currently in a relationship, this **10 reversed** could indicate that your client may be in denial about the health of the relationship. People who are used to struggling in relationships sometimes feel that the struggle *is love* and needs to be there. If perhaps your client has left or is leaving a relationship, this reversed 10 can bring a sense of real freedom and happiness.

26
ACE OF CUPS

(New Love or Passion about a New Project/Job)

ACE of CUPS.

The wonderful world of emotions! The element is water, and with water comes intuition.

This is the suit of expressing how we feel about ourselves and others, and the Ace of Cups is here to start the ball rolling into something brand new and passionate. It's the unique experience of love at first sight, the feeling of finally getting to work in the field you've been studying, or the special feeling you have seeing your child born. This is a joyous card and one of great promise. If your client is a single person and the question is about love, you can be confident they will be meeting someone new. This will not be someone blasting back from the past, but a new person they've never met or considered as a love partner. If the question is about love and your client is already in a relationship, it will indicate a deepening of that love, a new level of commitment.

Ace of Cups (new love/project) *before* the 2 of Cups (collaboration) indicates a love relationship or team project at work progressing well.

Ace of Cups (new love/project) coming *after* the 2 of Cups (collaboration) means a deepening in that partnership's commitment to each other, be it in love or business.

Ace of Cups (new love/project) and the 3 of Pentacles (internship) could mean finally being able to start working in your favored field of study.

Ace of Cups (new love/project) and the Devil (obsession) or reversed Moon (hidden agenda), or both, could be a covert or clandestine relationship. Eyes wide open; look for red flags.

Ace of Cups (new love) with the 4 of Cups (indifference) starts hot and then cools off. With Death (natural ending), it burns hot but burns completely out.

Ace of Cups (new love/project). It withers or becomes stale with the above cards but may be resurrected and revisited if you see the **Judgment card (rebirth)** anywhere in the lineup. Judgment doesn't reverse death often.

Ace of Cups (new love/project) with the **5 of Wands (gossip)** or the **5 of Swords (conflict/arguments)** means that this new beginning you had so much excitement about is hitting a rough patch. This combination doesn't mean the end of a new project or love. Many times, when people come together with deep emotions, everything feels like a fairy tale. But as we all know, we have to come back to reality sometime. If your relationship survives this inevitable turn of events, it can become stronger and mature successfully.

Ace of Cups (new love/project) with the **Lovers (physical love/collaboration)** usually means that a love relationship has reached a level of physical intimacy. It isn't often that this combination comes up when the partners haven't slept together, but it has happened. It does speak to the physical desires being quite strong. To be clear, this is when I'm reading for an established dating relationship. If the two people are not dating, just infatuated and flirting with each other, the presence of the Lovers card tells me the level of sexual tension and desire.

I read **Ace of Cups reversed** about the **same as upright**, depending on the question. If there was a fight, I may see this card reversed, but it doesn't mean the love isn't there. You may have a different experience, and I would enjoy hearing your thoughts on this.

㉗
TWO OF CUPS

(Partnership/Cooperation)

The 2 of Cups is the card that may indicate a collaboration with a passionate (Cups, feelings/emotions) focus on a person or project.

This is a card of mutual respect and common ground and harbors a feeling of equals or peers. This collaboration gives a person the awareness of high hopes and inspiration. If perhaps I'm reading for a client and the question is "Will I meet someone soon and start a great relationship?," this card will tell me that the great relationship looks quite hopeful, but most likely it will be with a person they already know.

This does not necessarily mean an ex-partner, although that could be the case; it is someone they have already been introduced to, at least once. When asking about work or money, it shows balance and harmony. It indicates working on a project with someone you enjoy being around, and the project progresses well.

The **2 of Cups reversed** does throw cold water on an otherwise awesome and hopeful collaboration but doesn't necessarily mean tragedy unless a few other dark actors (cards) create suspicion. I read it as a person not defining the relationship as a formal "both hearts looking at the same horizon" kind of thing. The relationship could grow into a 2 of Cups upright situation. Look at the accompanying cards. Oftentimes, I will be reading a lady who has decided, early on in a friendship, that the man isn't as emotionally invested as she is—that is, not yet. The reversed 2 of Cups cautions to bring her heart back to center, so the relationship stays balanced and grounded.

The **2 of Cups reversed** with the following, in any combination, gives me an uneasiness about where a relationship is going. **Devil (obsessions)**, usually sexually driven, with a possible tendency of ownership over the other, could develop into stalking behavior. The **5 of Swords (change/conflict)** or the **5 of Wands (gossip)** I call the bickering combination. Bickering and prodding each other, or one person, will trigger the other for "fun," but poking fun in a way that's derogatory and sarcastic. This craziness drives their partner to pull away. Once this happens, the one who is causing the arguments feels like a victim because the other couldn't take it anymore and left.

...

I find that this combination shows up when a client calls about just meeting someone and they have been out a couple of times. When I see some of the prior cards, I ask, "Did he or she talk about how bad their exes treated them?," and the answer is "Well, yes, they did." How people speak about their exes is how they will talk about you with their next love interest. Really keep your ears and eyes open when chatting with someone new. How they talk about the past will give you a clue on how they will talk about the moments you are sharing with them right now.

...

The **2 of Cups (partnership)**, **Moon (illusions)**, or **reversed Moon (hidden agendas)**. Upright or reversed, the Moon never shares their whole story. This card doesn't accuse a person of being dishonest, as some 5 cards do, but instead shares that this person isn't being completely open and forthright. I see this a lot on first dates both with men and women. Seeing these cards early in dating feels appropriate because you don't want to reveal everything about yourself in the first few dates; however, if a couple is established and I see the 2 and the Moon upright or reversed, I get concerned. Are they holding back because they are losing interest and closing down? The cards around this one will tell you the answer to that question.

If the **Death card (endings)** is hanging around, then I prepare my client to keep her feet on the ground and watch their heart, since their partner seems like they are slowly shutting the door. This can also indicate that something in that person's life has just ended, such as a project, contract, job, or friendship, and the reason why they may be quiet is that they are trying to adjust to the new circumstances. If the Death card is pointing to the death of the relationship, the only time I would find hope for a reunion is if the **Judgment card (resurrection)** shows up. Judgment is always good at stitching things back together, no matter how old or deep the wound is.

On a happier note, if the **2 of Cups (cooperative collaboration)** is leaning on the more cheerful side with possibly the **Hierophant (traditional values)**, it would tell me that the person I'm reading isn't afraid of marriage. If the **2 of Cups is upright** but the **Hierophant is reversed**, it means their person of interest isn't ready to talk about marriage or consider it right now. It can also indicate that a person never wants to marry again, but you would need to have other factors in the scenario, such as age and how long the couple has been together.

With the **3 of Cups (celebration),** there would be a call for a party celebrating the union. The 2 plus the 3 of Cups (**collaboration plus celebrations**) indicates a relationship progressing toward a deeper commitment.

When you see 2 of Cups with most Pentacles, then you can assume there's a sense of stability in the relationship. This is when you get proposals, rings, and weddings—you know, the tangibles. The cards to look for could be **Hierophant (traditional values)**, **10 of Pentacles (family/legacy)**, **7 of Pentacles (building a financial future)**, or **10 of Cups (domestic bliss)**.

The **2 of Cups (cooperative collaboration)** and the **2 of Pentacles (financial partnership)** show a good working relationship or intimate partnership that began at the workplace. Either they both work at the same place or they know their industries well.

The **2 of Cups (cooperative collaboration)** with the **Ace of Wands (new action)**, whether the union is for love or business, and the **2 or 3 of Wands (positive progression)** indicate things will be moving along well.

THREE OF CUPS

(Celebration with Friends and Community)

This is a fun one, since it suggests social interactions with celebrations.

This is the "Let's go for a beer after work" card. It's the "carefree group event where no one is excluded" card. If I'm reading for someone who is looking for a partner and the 3 of Cups comes up, they will, most likely, either meet someone at a group event or be introduced to a new love interest by friends. No matter where in the spread this card lands, it's meant to give an impulse to the recipient to get a group together to have some laughs or coordinate a night out with friends. These lighthearted gatherings are built into our lives for a reason. Let your hair down, have fun, and remember we are better together.

If the **3 of Cups (being social)** shows up in a business, career, or job reading, it means you will have profits through a group effort with shared interests.

The **3 of Cups reversed** can mean delayed plans and a feeling of being left out. We were all feeling a bit of that at the height of the lockdown, especially with the **Devil (obsessions/compulsions)**.

If I see the **9 of Cups (wishes/carefree)** and the **Devil (obsessions)** along with the **3 of Cups (socializing)**, there could be too much of a good thing. What starts as a fun social gathering may turn into a disappointment. Add the **Chariot (fast energy, usually road travel)** and we may have someone who might be drinking and driving. Rarely have I seen this combination when this hasn't been the case. Either this is the reason for an argument or something they are known to do.

The **3 of Cups (celebration)** upright or reversed with the **reversed 9 of Cups (wish card)** or the **Devil (obsessions/compulsions)**, or both reveal unhealthy compulsions or additions. If a client doesn't drink, it may mean this person is struggling with their sobriety.

The **3 of Cups (celebrations)** and the **Hierophant (traditional values)** point to a wedding. Putting in the **Lovers (physical love)**, **4 of Wands (solid foundations)**, or **10 of Cups (emotional fulfillment)**, or a combination of these, will strengthen the forecast.

If the **5 of Swords (conflict)** is anywhere near this awesome event, someone in the crowd is jealous and can't hide it.

FOUR OF CUPS

(Indifference, Distractions)

So as we move away from the party with the 3, we go into ourselves with the 4.

It's not a card that indicates alarming difficulty such as depression (it's only a 4), but a feeling more like an indifference about things. I have found this to be true when reading about love and relationships. This blah attitude means that boyfriends, girlfriends, spouses, et al. are not paying attention to the details or making the necessary effort to support the relationship or project. It doesn't necessarily mean they don't love you; it means they're being lazy. This card is a bit different if the topic is business, jobs, or money, since it can indicate a fixation on one thing to the exclusion of everything else.

I have discovered that for love, there is indifference for all things, and for money/job, there is indifference for everything except one. For a financial reading, there could be an overattachment to money and security.

The **4 of Cups (indifference)** is an interesting card because the surrounding suits will tell you what the problem is. In general, if there are positive cards before this one in a lineup, then whatever good fortune was there, the glory of it has worn off. Having positive cards before it means the event or prize just isn't holding this person's attention. That being said, if *after* this 4 come positive cards, there will be a bright breakthrough. You can tell what the person is struggling with when seeing what suit is around or after the 4 of Cups. If **Pentacles**, the disillusion or **loss of interest** will be **money** or a **job**.

Cups (emotion/love) mean disillusioned by heart connections, **emotions**.

Wands (actions) mean not motivated or interested in starting or finishing a project that needs **effort**.

Swords (thoughts) are lost and distracted by **disruptive thoughts**.

I've discovered that the reversed 4 of Cups is a bit like the upright, only a person tries hard to hide their indifference by acting interested, focused, and in sync with the group or team. This person is distracted by a thought or an emptiness. A cheerless despondency that hangs on the inside while the affected person pushes a smile through on the outside, so no one knows they are struggling.

The **4 of Cups (indifference)** with the **2 of Cups (collaboration)** shows that the person is not feeling close to partners, projects, or teammates. Love and affection have gone stale. This is only a 4 and is most likely a passing phase. Be aware of it but don't be attached to it, especially if the cards around are well aspected.

The **4 of Cups (indifference)** with **6 of Cups (old friends/family)**: distant feelings, not being available for friends. Add the **10 of Pentacles (family legacy)**: not being able to help the family or old friends.

If you have that **10 of Pentacles reversed**, it can show real harm to the emotional health of that family unit because of this person's inability to participate in family matters.

The **4 of Cups (indifference)** and the **Sun (success and pleasure)** highlight an inability to be grateful for what they have. One of the benefits of the Sun is self-expression. When a person is distracted by this 4, it's hard to acknowledge blessings. Keep in mind that whenever a big and bright major card sits next to a troubling card, the lesser does brighten up a bit. It's like the sun shines and lightens a person's spirit. Throw a colder major card such as the **Devil (obsessive brooding)** or **Tower (tearing down of the old)**, and it's like these cards splash negativity on all the other cards, making the 4 of Cups darker and gloomier.

The **4 of Cups (indifference)** with the **Hermit (withdrawal)** or even the **4 of Swords (rest)** means a person is wrapped up in their mind and desires solitude.

The **4 of Cups (indifference)** with certain other cards shows a deepening of the loneliness and can warn of a spiral into despair. Some cards to look for in this case would be the **Moon (illusions)**, **7 of Cups (options/some not balanced)**, **Devil (becoming obsessed)**, and **8 of Swords (feeling trapped)**. They all point to a more daunting side of this isolation and indifference.

FIVE OF CUPS

(Guilt/Remorse)

In most decks, the image shows a few cups tipped over and spilled, yet there are still two cups close by that are full. It's clear that there has been a disappointment about something. How the question is framed and the quality (positive/negative) of the cards around the 5 of Cups will point to what is causing the troubling feeling, along with the level of desperation regarding it.

If it's a love reading, someone is feeling bad about what was said or done. If it's work related, it's about not feeling fulfilled. This 5 is all about guilt and remorse. As distracting as these emotions can be, you need to remind your client that everyone makes mistakes, and with time, all will feel better. Many of us are so hard on ourselves, but I remember what Maya Angelou, the great American poet, wrote, in part: "We do our best and when we know better we do better." That sentence always helps me when I start treating myself badly with guilt and remorse.

When doing a love reading, if the client says, "We had a fight and I want to know how he's feeling about things," and I see the 5 of Cups, I say that he must care about them and the relationship because he feels bad about whatever was said or done. It's been my experience that, most likely, the remorseful person finds their way back into alignment with my client.

In a money/career/job reading, this card suggests you may incur further losses, and suggests reassessing your position. If it is a career, are you studying what you enjoy, or what will earn you the most money? Are you sacrificing contentment for cash? With regard to finances, have you invested in someone or something that is squandering your resources or taking you for granted? If asking about a job, there may be a better position out there if you look.

The **5 of Cups (guilt and remorse) reversed** isn't a complete turnaround from the upright meaning. I would put it as a half turn. This means the disappointment in themselves regarding their actions or decisions still burns, but they are standing up and moving forward with their lives. A person is over the worst of the crisis and figuring out how to make amends, or to move on. Again, look to the other cards to tell you which one they will be leaning toward.

Speaking of amends, if I see the **5 of Cups (guilt/remorse)**, **reversed or upright**, and followed by the **7 of Wands (defending position)** or the **8 of Swords (feeling trapped)**, then the person hasn't found the right words to mend the situation.

If this 5 is followed by the **8 of Cups (leaving a situation)** or **Death (natural endings)**, the person will most likely leave the relationship, job, or project as it stands and not come back to make amends.

Even if the **Judgment card (resurrection)** is in this reading, there will need to be a clean and clear break from the relationship or situation before that person could see clearly enough to negotiate a reunion.

...

If the 5 of Cups is in the future, no matter how bleak the prediction, it isn't real yet. It hasn't happened yet. This is a prediction only if the people involved stay the same, with the same attitude or devotion to conflict or actions. A prediction like the one prior is a warning that if everything stays the same, this would be the most probable future. A psychic reading is such a blessing because, with this information, the client can choose new actions, new words, and new strategies and will ultimately create a new and different future!

...

Another card that can indicate trouble with this 5 is the **3 of Swords (heartbreak)**. It's pretty common to see the **5 of Cups (guilt/remorse)** and heartbreak card. Again, nothing is set in stone, and with every hardship in a relationship, you are learning more about each other. If you see Court cards in this lineup, you can be sure that the reason for this guilt, remorse, and general hardship has to do with other people. In general, Court cards will show you the people who have participated in this struggle. If perhaps you see any reversed Court cards, this indicates people in your life who may be blocking the success of your relationship or project.

The **5 of Cups (guilt/remorse)** and the **4 of Swords (rest)** mean retreating from the situation to recover. Other cards will say how long it may take before progress is made.

The **5 of Cups (guilt)** and any of the lighthearted cards, such as the **Fool (welcome surprises)**, **Empress (pleasure)**, **Star (hope)**, or **Sun (happiness)**, or **Strength (grace under pressure)**. All speak to full recovery.

The **5 of Cups (guilt)** and **Temperance (diplomacy needed)**: must not overreact in this situation; stay calm.

The same is true when you have this 5 with the **Moon (illusions)**: not ready to be open with one another.

This 5 and **Tower (shattering/sudden changes)** will require a complete rebuilding of the relationship. The surrounding cards will tell you whether that person will put in the time and effort for the renewal.

The **5 of Cups (guilt)** with the **10 of Swords (betrayal)** complicates things. Look for other angry cards, such as the **5 of Swords (conflict/change)** or the **7 of Swords (cunning strategies)**, to understand what the future holds for this couple, whether romantic or business.

㉛
SIX OF CUPS

(Nostalgia/Renewal)

This card has everything to do with family and old friends. This is a regenerative card with refreshing memories of Mom's apple pie and family BBQs. It reminds us of our happy times from the past that brighten and lift our frequencies for a happier outlook for the future. It reminds us that we always have a home, even if that home is just a warm memory helping us move forward. One of the curious things I have found from my many readings is that if this particular card is dealt reversed, there is a feeling of separation from family and sometimes even a complete severing of ties from old friends as well. Remember, not every reversed card has the opposite meaning to the upright; however, it has been my experience that the reverse 6 of Cups representing a separation or a break from family/friends has been true.

In a love reading, **6 of Cups (family memory or visit from past)** could mean an old love coming back, but I would need to have another card on the table to back it up. When a client is asking if an old love they can't get over is coming back, this 6 is a good start. I would need to see **Judgment (resurrection)** or the **10 of Pentacles upright (solid past connection)** before I would mention it.

Let's explore this situation more closely. You have a client who is unable to get over a past love. You see the 6 of Cups in their reading, but no other cards that indicate the past love is coming back. The 6 can be telling you that the person you are looking at does have fond memories of your client. It also shows that the memory of your client occupies a special part of their heart. However, if I don't see more than the 6, I explain that I read energy signatures and impulses: "It shows that your loved one holds you in their heart and indeed has impulses to call now and again, but without stronger cards in the reading, I believe they talk themselves out of re-connecting." At that point, you can discuss different options they can take at the level of action that might catch this past love in a nostalgic mood and start communicating again.

The **6 of Cups (nostalgia/renewal)** and the **Knight of Wands (travel/moving)** may mean moving back to where you grew up. This could be a move of households or traveling for a visit with family and old friends.

The **6 of Cups (nostalgia/renewal)**, **3 of Cups (celebrations)**, and **8 of Wands (fast energy / air travel)** could be a last-minute reunion, graduation, or retirement party, and you will fly to attend.

The **6 of Cups (nostalgia/renewal)** and the **3 of Pentacles (new work / apprentice)** or the **8 of Pentacles (skill/determination)** could mean new work coming through someone you have known for years or moving back into work you used to do.

The **6 of Cups (nostalgia/renewal)** and the **Ace of Pentacles (starting a new business)** mean returning to a familiar place to start your business. Add the **2 of Cups (collaboration)** or the **Lovers (physical collaboration)** and you will be creating a new business with old friends or family members.

Where this 6 can lead you astray is when it is joined by some ungrounded cards such as the **Moon (illusion)** or the **7 of Cups (fantasy/imagination)**, and even the **High Priestess (emotions about inner life)**. They can sidetrack you to misremember the past and create an idealized story of what you thought happened.

The **6 of Cups (nostalgia/renewal)** together with our old friend the **Devil (obsessions/compulsions)** will have you unable to let go of a past love.

Anytime I have had this 6 with other family cards, such as the **Empress (divine feminine/mom)** and the **10 of Pentacles (legacy)**, or the **10 of Cups (emotional fulfillment)**, family and friends take center stage in someone's awareness. No matter when in the reading this shows up, it's usually a welcomed sight with a warm feeling.

㉜
SEVEN OF CUPS

(Fantasy, Imagination, Creativity)

 In most decks, this card has many beautiful cups floating in front of a lighthearted, giggling soul who has their choice of them. It indeed means that you have many options available to you. When this card shows up, it is telling you that not all those ideas and options are grounded in reality. The person you are reading for needs to do a bit more research or look for a new perspective before making a choice. It would help your client if they jotted down all their ideas and allowed you to read on each of them to help them separate the tangible, attainable ideas and those that are not so available at the time of the reading. Encourage your client to research everything before moving ahead or putting money on something. Have a second set of eyes look at the paperwork. Even consider waiting a week before they make up their mind. This will bring a higher chance of success and security in all of their projects.

The upright **7 of Cups (fantasy/imagination/creativity)** makes it clear that whomever this card is for, they don't have all the facts or are practicing spiritual escapism. Whether your reading is on love or money, you can be sure the people involved are not well informed. The reversed 7 is the opposite. Your client is focused and thinking clearly after a time of confusion.

The **7 of Cups (fantasy/imagination/creativity)** will be less risky when grounded cards are near it, such as the **Emperor (responsible/savvy)** or the **Hanging Man (open to other perspectives).** The Hanging Man means this person should entertain the thought that not all their ideas are viable. Whereas the Emperor indicates that even though there may be some fantasizing going on, this client still has one foot grounded in reality.

Any of the mature Court cards (Kings and Queens) around this 7, especially in the suit of Pentacles, will give enough assurance that this person's imaginative thinking isn't going to go far in regard to making poor choices with unfortunate consequences.

I have noticed that if this 7 is poorly aspected, with, let's say, either the upright or reversed **Magician (manifesting/manipulation)** or the **upright** or **reversed Moon (hidden agenda / illusion, with reverse being much worse)**, there is a person around likely spreading untruths. Someone could be eroding your client's understanding of reality by gaslighting or controlling them in some way.

It's appropriate to see this card when reading children or creative individuals who need this chamber of fantasy to produce their craft. This is not a bad or negative card. This is a wonderful card because it deals with the right side of our brains, the muse. Sitting in the power of imagination is the pathway to intuition and a necessary step when honing psychic skills. However, I do a lot of readings with people who are challenged by deep pain, and I don't encourage false hope. The fastest way out of your pain is understanding the facts of the situation. This will reveal the truth about yourself and what you've been saying "yes" to that you shouldn't be.

No path we walk is free from suffering, but the path a skilled advisor suggests with the knowledge available to them through clear sight will offer the least amount of pain and the quickest way to a peace-filled heart. If you find this hard to believe, then I challenge you to become a skilled advisor and experience this for yourself. You will be the gatekeeper to someone's better understanding of their situations and themselves. Nothing feels better than that.

33
EIGHT OF CUPS

*(Walking Away from a Person or Project You
Have Put a Lot of Time Into)*

The 8 of Cups is an empowering card for the person who receives it in a reading.

It indicates they have decided, on some level, to leave a situation or project that doesn't bring out the best in them anymore. It says they have put a lot of time and effort into it. Possibly they even looked at it as a lifetime commitment or investment, but the decision has been made to leave.

The perfect example is when you wake up one day and realize you can't stand your job or career choice. You went to school for it, worked to climb the ladder, and you can't do it any longer. The good part is that when this 8 shows up, the decision is made, and there is a sigh of relief that the challenge is over. It feels like a weight has been lifted off your heart, mind, and shoulders, and you are resolute. Suffering lives in the *decision-making*, not in the decision.

As an advisor, look to the proceeding cards to see what the seeker is walking away from: **Cups (emotion/love/passions)**, **Swords (spoken declarations)**, **Pentacles (money or property issues)**, or **Wands (walking away from the poor behavior of another)**.

If perhaps unfavorable cards follow this 8, such as the **5 of Cups (guilt and remorse)**, or if the **Devil** is around **(obsessions/compulsions)** or any quick-action card such as the **8 of Wands (fast action)**, it indicates there won't be much thought before walking away. Doing so may be premature or end in a regretful burst of emotion. The **5 of Swords (change/conflict)** can also indicate someone leaving without thought for others. Both the **8 of Wands (quick action)** and the **5 of Swords (arguments)** could point to a selfish, self-centered person walking away from the situation. The **10 of Swords (betrayal)** shows a reason why someone is walking away.

The **8 of Cups (walking away)** with the **2 of Wands (progressing collaboration)** or the **2 of Pentacles (financial collaboration)** is a combination I put into the category of business and not so much love. If the **2 of Cups** is present **(passionate collaboration)**, then the emotions of walking away, whatever the situation, are deep and may feel debilitating.

...

Do you remember a day or week, or longer, when you pondered a decision? It may have been to go to school or find work, or to join the military or a corporation. It could have been when to start a family, marry, or divorce. These are many of the struggles your clients will bring you. Remembering your own struggle will help you align and meet that person where they are. Remember that the conflicting thoughts take you right back to the feeling of sitting in the mud about the topic. After all the back and forth of imagining the future scenarios of each option, you finally decide. Right or wrong, the destination is set and you are waiting for life itself to mirror back how correct your choice was. This becomes a destiny point. And what a relief to be on your way instead of being stuck in indecision. The relief a person feels is remarkable.

When a person is resolved to a change, if doubt sneaks back in, their newly created declaration of truth pushes it aside. They anchor it with faith, and that's the end of it. That relief is what this 8 of Cups represents. The decision that brings peace, a path beyond uncertainty or misgiving. I like this 8 because it's so decisive. Even if you look back and discover a better choice could have been made, the feeling at the time is one of resolution and peace. That's when you know you are on the right track. Whatever choice you made carried important lessons.

...

③④
NINE OF CUPS

(Wishes/Celebration—Sometimes Called the "Bartender")

The 9 of Cups is a welcome card in the reading. This is the wish card. The card of joyful optimism, sharing with others through celebrations of all kinds. It bodes a generous nature of sincere goodwill. It has been my experience that in a general reading about someone's most probable future, this is a welcome card. However, I read for people in crisis, and that is how I teach this card. This card can indicate overindulging, overdrinking, or recreational drug use. How can I come to this conclusion? Because I once noticed that this card was reversed, and had a hunch that it meant her boyfriend used alcohol or drugs to cope, and then I just asked the client! I encourage you to query your clients when Spirit gives you a new idea about a specific card that gives you pause or a combination where you get an "idea" of what it would mean in your client's particular situation. As you work with your guides, they will offer insights that can be unique. I once had a client tell me that a spouse or loved one was struggling with alcohol and drugs. I saw the **9 of Cups (wish card)** in the reading and decided to look at this 9 as someone who may use drugs or alcohol as a coping mechanism.

If I get a call from an anxious spouse or partner wondering what their person is thinking and doing, and I see the **9 of Cups (even upright)**, I ask if their partner drinks. Almost every time they say yes or tell me their partner tends to overdo it. They may even tell me they are in recovery from the addiction. (When regarding a person in recovery, you never say they fell out of recovery; you tell them that their partner may be struggling with their sobriety). Have I been wrong? Well, a few times, but I discovered, after talking awhile, that when their partner is struggling, he throws himself into work or excessive exercise. So there is that component as well. The way to approach your client with this delicate topic is to be transparent. Take the time to say, "I have the reversed 9 of Cups in his reading, and most times when I have this card in this position it means he uses alcohol or recreational drugs to cope." If the answer is "No, not really; I've never seen him drunk," then I explain that he is either overworking or overindulging in a project that takes his mind away from the situation at hand. But most times, the *majority* of the time, the answer is yes. Their person tends to drink past fun and into intoxication.

A word of caution. If a client asks if their boyfriend has fallen off the wagon and started drinking, and I see this 9, I say they are struggling. It doesn't mean they are literally drinking. Same with the question about cheating. If I look behind their boyfriend's eyes and see the **Lovers (physical collaboration)**, it doesn't necessarily mean they are physically cheating. An advisor cannot differentiate among an emotional affair, a physical affair, flirting, or just thinking the waitress looks nice. Seriously. Reading energy doesn't allow such detail, so don't accuse a person of doing something that they most likely aren't doing. I would rather be wrong and say I don't see a cheater than be wrong by accusing an innocent person of something impossible for them to disprove to a frantic partner. Sometimes we pick up the insecurity of our client, and it spills into the reading. Don't match your client's energy. Stay neutral and centered, don't accuse anyone of anything, and don't speak in absolutes.

Upright **9 of Cups (wishes fulfilled)** indicates celebrations/party, and the **reverse 9** shows **overindulgence**. In a troubled-love reading, the reversed 9 of Cups shows that a person may be choosing destructive ways to cope with the situation. With the **9 of Cups (wishes fulfilled)** and the **Magician (easy manifesting),** you have the Midas touch. Everything seems to turn to gold. With the **9 of Cups (wishes)** and the **4 of Cups (indifference)**, you start off with a great idea, then give up, claiming it's too hard to achieve. Watch out—you will be manifesting more indifference. The **9 of Cups reversed (destructive indulgence)**, the **8 of Wands (fast-moving energy)**, and **Justice (contracts/law)** could mean legal consequences for your actions. The **9 of Cups reversed (destructive indulgence)** with either the upright or reverse **Chariot (travel)** could mean driving under the influence.

TEN OF CUPS

(Emotional Happiness)

The 10 of Cups is a statement of happiness and optimism for your family, extended family, and close friends. This shows that the person you are reading for has a profound sense of gratitude and well-being with life. If this card is placed in the future, then your client can enjoy the thought of grateful optimism heading their way. If they're having a hard time, this may be Spirit inviting you to shine the light on what they are grateful for, by naming off a few blessings they have coming in for them. Spirit is asking you to start the reading there, at gratitude. It's a time to acknowledge that sense of belonging we enjoy when remembering there are friends and family who care and want the best for us.

As with all 10s, it signifies a conclusion, and you collect the bounty of your actions for this cycle. And like all other 10s, if reversed it shines the light on choices or behaviors that didn't serve you well. Whatever topic you are discussing with your client, if a 10 of any suit comes up, it shows the ending and assessment of that topic. If reversed, it gives you an idea of how your client is feeling about themselves and others regarding the subject.

The **10 of Cups reversed** shows **disappointment and discontent**. Cups are emotions, all emotions. Disappointment is an emotion stemming from sadness. Regarding money, this reversed 10 tells you to scale down your expectations, expenditures, and even your lifestyle. Simplify life; declutter and back up from self-imposed obligations until you feel the thankfulness return. What you are bringing in isn't aligning with your idea of success. Regarding your job, this card reversed shows problems with the company or insecurity with your position. Reading about love, this reversal shows a partner who may not be sharing the same value or ideas regarding family. It could mean not getting along with close family members, in-laws, and stepchildren, to name just a few. Upright, this 10 speaks volumes about how well you've done and how you're continuing to prosper and grow a good life. Be it work, job, career, family, or love, things look bright.

As far as combinations, I could list many, but this card is so straightforward I need to name just a few.

The **10 of Cups (emotional fulfillment)** and the **Hierophant (traditional values)** mean a wedding or marriage is close.

The **2 of Cups (passionate collaboration)**, **Hierophant (traditional values)**, and this 10 mean proposals and marital bliss. **Reversed 10 of Cups (disappointment)** with this doesn't necessarily mean you are not going to enjoy a happy wedding or marriage proposal, but does point to the fact that your *expectations* are out of line with reality. I see this card reversed in love readings around major holidays, because people feel it so romantic to be proposed to at Christmas or New Year's, and other times such as birthdays and Valentine's Day. It can be hard to keep pace with your partner when you hope they are in your future the way you picture it. And the reversed 10 of Cups may be showing that the picture you have in your heart is setting you up for disappointment and blocking a different, possibly more romantic, blessing that may be available through your partner.

The **10 of Cups (emotional fulfillment)** in a reading about your job signals that rewards, respect, and recognition are coming.

Before going on to the Pentacles, I want to highlight something important. Relationships live inside the suit of Pentacles, not the suit of Cups. Cups are all about emotion, this is true, but you can't hold emotion in your hand. You can hold a relationship, with all its declarations of truth, marriage certificates, and the various phases of a relationship, in a tangible way. How? The obvious marriage certificates, the court system documents, and the different phases of a relationship are actionable. For instance, as just friends, your assumptions and expectations are different than if you have declared your relationship exclusive. Same when the next step is fiancé or fiancée. Each phase holds different actions that manifest as things in the world. Pentacles are things.

36
ACE OF PENTACLES

(New Financial Avenue or Acquisition)

ACE of PENTACLES.

The Ace of Pentacles (material) is the beginning of something tangible. Unlike with **Cups (emotion)**, **Swords (thought)**, or **Wands (action)**, you can hold a Pentacle. It's the money in your pocket, the car you drive, the person you live with, and the certificate on your wall—all the stuff you can touch and hold.

...

A good way to remember the difference in energies is this: a guitar you can hold in your hands since it's tangible (Pentacle), but the thought that went into writing the music (Swords) and the level of emotion that was expended while singing the song (Cups) while strumming the strings (Wands, action) during the performance are not tangible. You can't hold the sound of a song, or the emotion or the action of singing in your hands. The tangible and intangible together make for a beautiful and holistic experience.

...

For a love question, this Ace may mean the two met through work, or they are familiar with the other's industry. It could also mean going into business together, but you will need to see other cards around this Ace to hold that assumption. For money/career/job questions, this Ace means new investments or opportunities. If for a job, it could indicate a brand-new job or a new position in the same company. It can also symbolize a raise or promotion. The **Ace of Pentacles reversed** doesn't describe the opposite per se but will point to **insecurities about money** or obsessive greed. One will feel out of balance, such as with hoarding and overattachment to an outcome.

Ace of Pentacles reversed with the **Fool card (unexpected lucky breaks)** will point to missed opportunities. The Fool should be close to the Ace to mention something like that. Also, the placement of the Fool will tell you if the opportunity was missed in the past or a new opportunity is in the future, and the most likely outcome will be that they will dismiss a new opportunity. Again, the benefit of forecasting the future is to encourage someone to have eyes to see an incoming blessing. It may just change their lives greatly.

...

There's a reason why your client has asked for a reading today. Think of all the things that had to sync up to have you and your client talking. They had to have found you and decided to call and form their questions. All the studying you have done was to prepare to read for this person and your ability to hear spirit through the cards. Life is bigger; you are bigger than you realize.

...

Ace of Pentacles reversed (financially insecure) with the **5 of Pentacles (poverty mentality)** regarding job/career will show a level of frustration, feeling stuck at the workplace (**the Ace**) and overspending on weekends to make up for the emotional dissatisfaction (**the 5**).

Ace of Pentacles reversed for love can describe a relationship built on money, security, and how things look to others rather than true love.

Ace of Pentacles (new financial pathway) and love cards such as the **Lovers (physical collaboration)** or the **2 of Cups (passionate collaboration)** and **Hierophant (traditional values)** mean joining resources as a live-in situation (more at the beginning of a relationship) or the step toward being committed to marriage, or the love in a marriage deepening.

Ace of Pentacles (new financial pathway) and the **6 of Wands (recognition)** mean promotion, advancement, or certificate of achievement. If the **3 of Pentacles (apprentice / good work)** is close, it shows the same as above but to a lesser degree.

Ace of Pentacles (new financial pathway) and the **3 of Wands (merchant / trade and commerce)** shine a light on profits improving. Trust your intuition on buying and selling.

Ace of Pentacles (new financial pathway) sitting next to the very generous **6 of Pentacles (charity/philanthropy)** indicates an opportunity to change someone's life by either giving something needed or receiving something that changes you for the better.

Along those same lines, the **Ace of Pentacles (new path)** with the **8 of Pentacles (passionate study)** means a course of study you really enjoy, such as when indulging in a hobby for possible profit is available. Add the **6 of Pentacles (generosity/philanthropy)** and I would feel confident saying that the course of study would be paid for by others.

③⑦
TWO OF PENTACLES

(Financial Partnerships / Balancing Budgets)

The 2 of Pentacles is the proverbial balancing act of budgets, savings, and possessions.

Because it's a 2, with its duality, we have to remember there might be someone else involved, someone helping you out on a financial level or supporting your well-being on a practical level. If the reading is about money and finances, it's an acknowledgment of juggling your resources well. You aren't feeling all that rich, but you're not all that poor either. If perhaps it's a love reading, someone looking for love, this 2 is another card that points to meeting someone at work or someone who knows the client's industry well. If perhaps the client is already in an established relationship, this card could be signaling a collaboration on a project or business and prospering.

The **2 of Pentacles reversed** does mean the opposite of the upright. Instead of balancing budgets and happy financial partnerships, you need to protect yourself from duplicitous backhanders. The difference is really stark with this 2. **Upright is trust**; the **reverse is don't trust**. If faced with the 2 of Pentacles reversed, and you have no way out of a project, make sure you document and verify steps, and any promises need to have written backup attached.

A love reading:

The **2 of Pentacles (financial collaboration)** and the **2 of Cups (emotional collaboration)** show a joining of resources, such as moving in together. Add the **4 of Wands (building a firm foundation)** and you could be looking at purchasing a house together. Throw down the **Hierophant (traditional values)** and you are talking about a deeper commitment such as marriage.

The same cards for money/job look like this:

The **2 of Pentacles (financial collaboration)** and **2 of Cups (emotional collaboration)** mean joining resources on a shared business plan or group effort. Add the **4 of Wands (building a firm foundation)** and that shared vision has a solid, stable presence. If the **Hierophant (traditional values)** shows up, your enterprise will be recognized as an industry standard-bearer.

Sidenote: The difference between the Hierophant and the Emperor

The Hierophant and the Emperor do about the same thing. They both represent traditional values, tactics, and strategies. As a rule, the Hierophant is about traditional religious institutions and norms while the Emperor is about traditional corporate rules, regulations, and norms. Same power, different focus. If I have the Hierophant in a reading about money and finance, I will treat it as the Emperor as far as business standards and practices, with the assumption that the business is, most likely, rooted in a deep ethical ethos and fair trade or is focused on community wellbeing.

...

The **2 of Pentacles (tangible partnership)** poorly aspected with the **5 of Swords (change/conflict)** or **7 of Swords (illusion and tricks)** means to treat this 2 as if it's reversed, and to check out where your money is, to be sure everything is on the up and up. A negative card around this delicately balanced 2 is signaling caution to your client.

The **2 of Pentacles (tangible partnership)**, the **Justice card (contracts)**, or the **Wheel of Fortune (luck improving)** and **Fool (lucky breaks)** could mean a nice lottery win. Something that more than one person has participated in with the same focus, which for me is the lottery but could be a competition at work or gaming/sports.

③⑧
THREE OF PENTACLES

(Creativity/Self-Expression/Skill)

This 3 shows that you are very good at what you do creatively or in your chosen career path. It's the signature of an artisan. Whenever I see the 3 of Pentacles, no matter what the topic of the reading, I take a moment to remind my clients that spirit is sharing with me that they are very good at what they do. People notice and aspire to do things more like them. It's work ethic and diligence that show up when you're a novice destined for journeymen in short order. The difference between this card and the **6 of Wands (being noticed / standing out)** is that the amount of time on the job is greater. And this 3 makes it clear you offer more creativity, and the 6 of Wands makes sure people notice your excellence.

The **3 of Pentacles (skill/creativity)** for a love reading shows a willingness and desire to build a solid relationship. This can be for friendships as well. A person with this 3 in their reading has great follow-through with friends and family alike, as well as quick wit and good communication.

With the **3 of Pentacles (creative skill)** and the **6 of Wands (being noticed)**, you are most likely in store for a promotion (add a major card, and that position might be upper management).

The **3 of Pentacles (creative skill)** and **8 of Pentacles (focused study)** mean apprentice to journeyman quickly.

The **3 of Pentacles (creative skill)** with the **10 of Wands (uneven workload)** or the **9 of Wands (ready to give up)** means an overstressed situation. However, if the **Devil is close (obsessive/compulsions)**, you may be a highly competitive person or a workaholic, bringing hardships and struggle on yourself.

The **3 of Pentacles (creative skill)** on its own is a great card. Add the can-do attitude of the **Magician (magical abilities and hidden power)** and you can create miracles. This means that the book you want to write or the program or video course or the blog just flows out perfectly. A good time to ride the creative wave with this combination.

The **reversed 3 of Pentacles** means you may not be at your best. I've discovered that this negativity is an inside job. Meaning, there is a lack of confidence in your own abilities, or life isn't offering the opportunity to showcase your abilities. The reversed 3 doesn't say that you don't have talent and skill. It does, however, speak to the doubt you have in yourself, or acknowledges that you're trapped in a situation where you don't have the prospects or forum to create.

The **3 of Pentacles (creativity/skill)** with the **Hermit (quiet solitude)** means you won't be showcasing or broadcasting your skills and abilities. As mentioned above, if the **6 of Wands (being noticed)** is close, you won't have to brag to others about your abilities. They will be either announced by others or quietly witnessed and noted for later.

The **3 of Pentacles (creativity/skill)** and the **8 of Swords (feeling trapped)** mean you have set aside your desire to create new experiences, projects, friendships, and love relationships because of something you feel is holding you back. This might show a pulling back from your own desires so as not to trouble another (usually family obligations), or in fear that you may lose something if you self-indulge. The **8 of Swords (feeling trapped by circumstances)** says you are declaring there isn't a way to showcase your talents. People do this when they think that if they follow their muse, it might interrupt the desired lifestyle. Or to follow their creative spirit isn't culturally acceptable. This would be evident if the **6 of Cups (family and friends from long-ago past)** or the **10 of Pentacles (legacy/inheritance)** was in the spread as well.

The **3 of Pentacles (creativity/skill)** with the **Death card (natural endings)** means that an outlet may be closing and a new one opening. Unlike the above scenario, where a person puts themselves in jail without creative options, life asks you to stop and start something old in a new way.

㊴
FOUR OF PENTACLES

(Cautious Security)

The 4 of Pentacles is sometimes interpreted as someone being greedy or holding back their money negatively. I don't see it that way. Through my years of reading for others, I've discovered that this card represents a person who has been in lack and is now living just above the waterline regarding financial comfort. The image of this card in many decks may show someone hiding four coins, looking like they are hoarding, but it's clear to me that this person knows where all their resources are by keeping close track of it all. It has nothing to do with being greedy or stingy, but a practical card that shows smart management of resources. The only time I would see this card as a negative is if the obsessive Devil was close, because that always brings excessive and over-the-top compulsions. The 4 of Pentacles reversed is someone afraid of losing—again. This isn't the first time they've recovered from lack. If your client has been suspended in this energy for a long while, then you can start describing this reversed 4 as clinging to poverty mentality and possibly stagnation. But be careful—that isn't a very nice thing to say when someone is struggling. Better to point out things they do have that support them instead of saying they are poverty minded. It's a tricky dance: on the one hand, you want to be open, but the other seems too harsh. Err on the positive side, and if this combination shows up and you feel that the information won't be received with an open mind, then skip it altogether.

If your client doesn't have a problem with a poverty mindset and is involved with a financial transaction, then the reversed 4 is suggesting they retreat from the investment in question. The project or prospect is not in their best interest. The most likely reason would be eventually losing control of the situation, project, or team.

The **4 of Pentacles (cautious security)** with the **Fool (lucky breaks)** and the **8 of Swords (feeling trapped)** means they may be shying away from an unexpected but wonderful opportunity and are afraid to let go of something that isn't working anymore. There's a wonderful list of well-aspected cards. Here are a few:

The **4 of Pentacles (cautious security)** followed by the **7 of Pentacles (financial improvement)** means putting a little aside for the future. But a perfect lineup would look like this: **5 of Pentacles (overspending)** to **4 of Pentacles (mindful of your money)** to **7 of Pentacles (financial improvements/savings)** . . . then, let's flip it around:

Let's say the 4 of Pentacles comes first, which is being mindful of your money; then you overspend with the 5 but get back on track with the 7. As long as the 7 is at the end of the reading, then however your client is handling their money will be okay. The 5 says they may overspend a little, but not enough to be a problem.

The **4 of Pentacles (cautious security)** and the **Empress (power and abundance)**: **Strength (grace under pressure)** persevering will pay off. Dot all the I's and cross all the Ts, and you will succeed.

The **4 of Pentacles (cautious security)** and the **following** all are good news.

Wheel of Fortune (good times coming). Stay the course and life will automatically turn more prosperous. You don't have to do anything different.

Sun (happiness and success). Bright opportunities are right in front of you. Keep aware and get ready to say yes to new things coming.

World (triumphant in the present cycle) results are much like the Sun card **above**.

The **10 of Cups (emotional fulfillment)**. This 10 will lift all burdens. This means no matter what your situation, happiness is available.

All the prior combinations point to better days ahead. Except for the 10 of Cups, which means you aren't waiting for better days to come, you can live happily ever after now. Some cards can quicken this promise of good fortune. For instance, if one or more cards in the suit of Wands make an appearance, manifesting tends to speed up.

I Just Lost My Job!

Give Awesome Readings

Client: "I just lost my job; I'm getting some unemployment but not enough to cover my monthly expenses. Tell me there's a job coming soon." (The cards are bolded in the throw that follows, and my thought process is in the parentheses. What I actually say to the client is summed up at the end.) Follow along the train of thought and see how the reading takes shape. The cards, in the beginning, don't necessarily hold true for what's to come. Aside from a question or two from me, the advisor, only to ensure a good frame of reference, hold your thoughts until the last card is on the table.

The **8 of Wands (situation)** indicates that this was an out-of-the-blue event she didn't see coming. (This is information for me, not so much for the client, but it does inform how shocking the situation is. I can really understand her surprise.)

The **5 of Pentacles (influencing situation)**. She has been overspending? Wonder if her overspending is out of necessity, like for an emergency of some kind, or if she has a habit of living outside her means? This card points to a simple overspending and not a big issue. More cards will answer our questions; no need to ask the client anything just yet.

Tower (how she feels on the inside) predicts that her lifestyle and spending will need to be completely restructured to be able to handle the situation. Because it is a Major card, this is the first indication that her new job is not right around the corner. The Tower brings big change, and the changes need to stand for freedom and peace. But I don't reveal that just yet in the reading. I need confirmation about this in the following cards, but this is a strong pointer to a longer unemployment time than she will be wanting to hear.

As mentioned earlier, I've learned NOT to start talking about the predictions until all the cards are on the table. I've messed up readings when I feel the pressure to give information, and I talk about each card as it's turned. The reading often sounded convoluted and confusing when I did that. The reason is, not every card you lay down will be information for your client. Much of the information is for you, the advisor, to better understand your client and what they need to hear, and, most importantly, how they process information.

The **4 of Pentacles (what she shows on the outside)**. She has a good idea where her money is and how it should be spent, making the above Tower card a bit stronger. I may need to tell her that her financial comfort level will be challenged. So this is the second card that tells me a new job might not be around the corner. But I say nothing. We need the whole picture by continuing the throw.

The **4 of Cups (what happened in the last thirty days that influences this situation)**. Interesting card because it means, in general, indifference, not paying attention to details. I'm not sure how this card plays into the reading yet. This might just be what I call a placeholder—a card that doesn't fit in a reading but needs to take that place, so the following cards are in the right order.

So far the reading has told me the way she lost her job (quickly and out of the blue), as well as what her financial situation is. She is mindful of her money and doesn't spend extravagantly. But what about that Tower? The restructuring of everything around her. Then the 4 of Pentacles, with its mindfulness of money. Is the Tower, the complete crumbling of her finances, a prediction of her future? Or is Spirit telling me she feels panicked about a catastrophic collapse of all financial security and *her fear is spilling into the reading*? Is our Tower something real, a caution? Or has her level of anxiety about the future reflected on the table? The following cards tell me how to approach this reading.

Sun (direct future) means bright future ahead. This card brightens the darkness our Tower brought in earlier. Judgment means that someone from the past will call with options. Or, someone from the past will pop into her mind, provoking an impulse to contact this person from her long-ago past. This card also tips the hat toward a history of good stewardship regarding her resources = 4 of Pentacles.

The **2 of Pentacles (how she views herself)** means balanced finances and affairs. So things may be tight, but everything will be covered. She mentioned in her question about not having enough to make ends meet with just the money from unemployment, but this card along with

Judgment (environment) (help from the past), either from her own savings or from friends, plus it shows she has built up good relationships with creditors that she can leverage.

Devil reversed (hopes and fears) means she's mindful of her obsessiveness on matters of money and possibly habits she may have with drinking to excess or other coping activities, overeating, overspending when sad, hoping some purchase will make her feel better. Again, this card is information for me about how my client thinks and feels about her situation. The upright Devil would indicate she may choose poor ways of coping with the situation, but reversed tells me she is self-aware and knows what to do.

King of Cups (most likely outcome) tells me she isn't as alone as she may be feeling, and speaks to the **Judgment** card earlier. Our King is, most likely, a father or father figure who will help out if needed. This King is our last card in the Celtic Cross spread, but I modify it a bit. If the last card is not a Major Arcana, I keep laying down cards, each representing 30 days, to see how long this phase will last. I put only a few cards down, however, and if I don't have a Major card in the next four or five turns, I quit with that theory. The reason is because the farther you get away (timewise) from the reading, the less likely that your trajectory will be correct. The first few months I'm quite confident, but farther out, there are so many opportunities to make new choices that the prediction is fruitless.

The next card is The **World**, which, timingwise, came through within a couple of months. The World is so comforting because it says she will be triumphant in her search for a new job. It also shows that the job will be a much better fit. Almost like Spirit saying that losing your job was the only way we could get you into something better.

This is how I gave the reading:

Me: "I'm so sorry to hear you lost your job, and you're so afraid. I can tell how the news hit you hard and **fast** (**8 of Wands**), which caused panic imagining all sorts of **hardships** (**Tower**), but I'm seeing all good things for your future (**Sun and World**). First, because you have nurtured your past relationships (**Judgment**), not just with friends and family but your **creditors** (**King of Cups**), by being responsible for your financial commitments (**4 of Pentacles**), you will find a lot of support just by letting people know your situation. A father, or father figure (**King of Cups**), who can also be a landlord or creditor, will be a big help. This man is kind and will comfort you, so you won't feel so afraid. After you get back on your feet, which looks to be quite soon, with a better job, you may want to spend some time restructuring your finances (**Tower**) only to feel better prepared emotionally if something like this happens in the future. You mentioned you don't have enough to cover expenses, but Spirit is saying you do. Your expenses will be covered (**2 of Pentacles**) either by having enough to pay yourself or through the kindness of others helping. Both the **Judgment** and **World** cards tell me you have friends in your industry or whom you have known since childhood who can help with your next position. Don't panic; just inform people you are looking; don't give in to your obsessive nature to worry (**Devil**), and allow people to help."

She relaxed, called some friends, and was back to work sooner than two months, and yes, making more money. If she had spent most of the first month frantic about her situation, the solution may not have been able to be realized sooner than predicted.

FIVE OF PENTACLES

(Poverty Mindset)

In most decks, the image on this card shows a couple or family who is sad and empty handed.

Remember, this is a tangible suit, so it represents a client feeling in lack. Yet, all they would have to do is turn around and see the light and warmth coming from the building behind them. This card means a person has been overspending. If this card was in a future position, it might be indicating that a strong impulse to overspend is coming.

Remember that people get psychic readings to figure out what their most probable future is, knowing that forewarned is forearmed. However, I need to remind you that this is only a 5 and doesn't represent catastrophic situations. Still, you should pay attention to it because, over time, overspending small amounts can lead to bigger problems. By all means, if you're in a pinch and need a hand, don't be afraid to ask for help from others. Inform friends and family of your situation and allow the universe to provide.

The **5 of Pentacles reversed** shows recovery from setback.

The **5 of Pentacles upright (poverty mindset)** close to the **7 of Swords (illusion/trickery)** may point to someone taking advantage of you.

This **5** with the **9 of Swords (worry)** shows mental distress so out of control that a person is losing sleep over a situation.

The **5 of Pentacles (poverty minded)** with the **9 of Pentacles (financial security)** points to good fortune and security. Certainly a welcome combination.

The **5 of Pentacles (poverty minded)** with the **reversed Justice (contracts)** can mean loss due to a legally binding commitment. If this reversed Justice is in the future, trace back to where the client accepted the deal, and work at understanding the situation from there. Many times, by going backward to find the root cause of the challenge, new pathways to correct a detail before it becomes a problem are indicated.

The **5 of Pentacles (poverty mindset)** with well-aspected cards such as the joy-filled **Sun (success)** and **Temperance (steady and even actions)** points the way out of hardship.

SIX OF PENTACLES

(Generosity)

The spirit of the card is one of generosity, and, for the most part, people who have this card in their readings have the resources to be generous either with money or the gift of their time.

There have been a few times I've read for someone who has a **6 of Pentacles (generous, spirit)** with the **5 of Pentacles (in lack)** bank account. Those are the people who *do* for others instead of giving money. They are the ones to pick up kids from school to help you out, make dinner when you don't have the time, or simply make sure you know they are available whenever you need them. Pentacles, tangible acts of affection and care. You don't have to be rich to feel rich and have the impulse to be of benefit to others. This is balance and harmony with the desire that all can have equally. In a legal reading, this card indicates mediation over judge and jury.

The **6 of Pentacles (generosity)** with the **Empress (feminine power and abundance)** points to community service and donations. Another example would be paired with the **Hierophant (traditional values)**, which would be formal church activities and fundraisers. Both The **Empress (as Mother Nature)** and **Hierophant (religious patriarch)** are conservators to worthy social concerns that include being conscientious witnesses to child and animal welfare causes.

The **6 of Pentacles (generosity)** alongside the **5 or 7 of Swords (conflict and illusion)** could mean your generosity is being taken advantage of.

The **6 of Pentacles (generosity)** with the **8 of Swords (feeling trapped)** means you are either feeling obligated to contribute through pressure from others or, possibly, you are obsessed with making people think you have more than you do. Usually, the latter will have more disruptive cards close by, such as the **7 of Cups (Illusions)** or, believe it or not, the **6 of Wands (being noticed for good work)**. Not often do I see the 6 of Wands in a negative light, but I have, on occasion, figured out that my client enjoys self-promotion.

SEVEN OF PENTACLES

(Financial Growth on a Personal Level)

The **7 of Pentacles** gives a feeling of accomplishment for your efforts.

In most decks, you will see a person in casual working clothes, holding a shovel, tending to what seems to be a money tree. When you see this card, Spirit is telling you to acknowledge the hard work the client has invested in the topic, since it shows concern about saving and growing wealth.

When I see this card in a love reading, Spirit is saying how much time and effort your client has put into cultivating the relationship. Tilling the ground to create firm footing for a healthy, progressive partnership. If in a reading about money, because this is **Pentacles (material)**, it suggests that the person you are reading has invested successfully in long-term, slow growth investments that compound profits.

This is self-made money or money set aside to ensure personal security. Don't get it confused with the **10 of Pentacles (family money/inheritance)**, which is money you may receive that you haven't personally earned.

The apprenticeship with the **3 of Pentacles** is slow and takes time to get to journeyman status. The **4 of Pentacles** shows *slow but steady* acquisition and careful placement of your wealth to ensure future prosperity. It all takes time and patience. The **7 of Pentacles** takes time as well. A little in the bank from each paycheck and rounding up to add to savings builds slowly but surely. That's the nature of this suit.

The **7 of Pentacles (financial growth)** with the **Empress (Mother Nature)** as well as **10 of Pentacles (family legacy)** leads to a business curated off the land and handed down through generations.

If **7 of Pentacles (financial growth)** is together with the **6 of Cups (old friends and family)** along with the **Ace of Pentacles (new business)** or **2 of Pentacles (financial collaboration)**, you may be starting a new business with a legacy or endowment in mind.

The **7 of Pentacles reversed** is an obvious lack of savings or resources, if the reading is for money or a job. If the reading is about love, the **7 of Pentacles reversed** is someone feeling that the time put into a relationship may not have taken hold or grown into something lasting. This insecurity can be real or imagined. This is how to decide which it is.

The **7 of Pentacles reversed** with the **7 of Cups (fantasy/imagination)**. I would say that the insecurity your client is feeling is, most likely, all in their mind. Another indicator of unnecessary worry is the **9 of Swords (overthinking)**.

Whether the **7 of Pentacles reversed** indicates a real problem is if the **10 of Pentacles (legacy/inheritance)**, **Tower (restructure needed)**, and most all other cards in the Pentacle suit show, because of their tangibility.

Having enough money is subjective and different for everyone. I was reading a millionaire one afternoon (I knew he was a millionaire only because he told me so). He was a bit of a braggart, but I learned the amount of money he had liquid and the assets he owned, included a golf course in the South. Several years prior, his family business (run by his father at the time), **10 of Pentacles (Legacy)**, applied and received a government contract, thus enabling them to deliver items they manufactured in their small business to help with a catastrophic disaster. Their family had exclusive rights over that one commodity, which made the whole family millionaires overnight. The entire family went to work full-time manufacturing this item. My client and his siblings stopped their outside jobs and schooling to dedicate themselves to fulfilling the contract. They worked around the clock for weeks, and it all paid off. After the contract was fulfilled, all he had to do was manage his money well and he wouldn't have to work another day in his life.

This reading found him in a panic. First thing he said was "I'm broke! I think my wife is going to leave me. I have only $500K in my checking account!" I couldn't help myself and tried hard (without a crazy expression) to realign his thinking to the fact that no one who has $500,000 in their checking account, not to mention all the other assets, is broke. But really, I was wrong. Not factually wrong, but in assuming his comfort level with that amount, because I was using *my* measuring stick, not his. I regretted showing my hand with my agenda, but he didn't flinch. Because he is such an open guy, not afraid to talk about personal matters with everyone, he seemed immune to quick retorts from people. Wealth and success, in general, are a mindset and not verified by facts and figures. It doesn't matter how much you have when you're in the grip of fear. Emotions are so powerful.

So when you see the reversed **7 of Pentacles (losing savings)** during a reading, it could be best to say that "it looks like you may feel insecure about resources," then let them tell you the specifics if they want to. If your insight doesn't trigger a problem, then work your way backward (in the throw) to see where the strain might be. Perhaps the **5 of Pentacles (overspending)** or the **Devil (indulging in addiction)** is causing the problem. If the **Tower (destruction of the old)** is before this **reversed 7 of Pentacles**, it points to a major restructuring in life and possibly a struggle rebuilding.

㊹
EIGHT OF PENTACLES

(Focus/Study)

This 8 reflects a maturity regarding a person's ability to create wealth, mainly because of a great work ethic. Reflecting on how the number makes a difference, take for instance the **3 of Pentacles (apprentice)**, the student. It shows the novice studying the craft, while the **8 of Pentacles** is the **journeymen**, the teacher. This is a good card to look for when reading someone looking for work. **The Ace of Pentacles (new avenue of income)** and the **Knight of Pentacles (stable business pathway and money)** can shine additional positive light for employment.

The **reversed 8 of Pentacles** speaks about the hamster wheel many of us feel we are on when working full time but not having the feeling of getting ahead. This can show maxing out credit cards and paying the minimum on bills.

Are you not earning enough, or are you living beyond your means? At **work**, the **reversed 8** mentions that the grind is **wearing you down**. In **love**, it's **waning affection**. Again, to better understand which one is the block and to find the restriction, reverse engineer the reading. Retrace the card lineup and start with the dominant suit, if there doesn't seem to be a spotlight on the specific cause. Pentacles, money and asset mismanagement. Wands, not feeling free to take action. Cups, deep emotions possibly holding you back from participating in material matters. Swords could be that you are overthinking the situation and being over-cautious, which freezes you in one very uncomfortable spot. If you don't have enough cards on the table to look back, then reshuffle and create a new throw with that specific question.

The **8 of Pentacles (focus/study)** with the **6 of Wands (being noticed)** along with **5 of Wands (competition)** indicates a group effort of some kind, possibly a contest or fundraiser. This 8 is all about doing what fulfills you. Something you are passionate about.

The **8 of Pentacles (new study)** and any **ace** suggest new work or a new project you will be happy and successful with.

The **8 of Pentacles (new study)** coupled with the **8 of Wands (fast action)** means you will advance quickly with whatever you are indulging in. Your level of curiosity coupled with your desire to be proficient pays off with this magical combination.

The **8 of Pentacles (new study)** and any of the corporate cards, **Hierophant (religious traditions)** or the **Emperor (corporate traditions and norms)**, show success with white-collar, higher-education industries. If, however, you have the **King of Swords (military man)** or the **Knight of Swords (uniformed careers)**, then blue-collar or physically active industries, such as law enforcement, would fit well. Consider if (still focusing on the 8) there was the **King/Queen of Pentacles** or the **Knight of Pentacles**, which points to a career in finance, at any level.

This is the card that will help you manifest work and profits around what you love to do. Study and enjoy learning everything you can, so you can use that skill to create your own business or propel you to new levels working for others.

There are many options that Spirit has to get the right information to you. Not only from the direct meaning of each of the 78 cards, but the story you put together combining other cards. Reading the Tarot is like learning how to put together an awesome puzzle while you, the advisor, can rework the edges as needed, through your intuition and life experience to support and serve another well.

ⓐ45
NINE OF PENTACLES

(Material Security and Well-Being)

This beautiful card shows a deep feeling of satisfaction, well-being, comfort, and success.

You have what you need and most everything you want. This is a time to enjoy your hard work and a time of plenty. It's a job well done and goals achieved.

You have a reason to be proud of yourself and can stand on your own, showing independence and sovereignty. This is the card I see most often with clients who are comfortable with or without a partner. There is a lot of emotional freedom in that, and I hope everyone gets to enjoy what that feels like sometime in their lives. Nothing else feels quite like being financially secure in the world all by yourself.

That being said, the reversed 9 doesn't mean you don't have what you want, but points to your material security being provided by another.

Another combination that points to insecurity (even if this 9 is upright on your table) is the **9 of Swords (worry)** or the **8 of Swords (feeling trapped)**, or both. Many people are living with what appears on the outside as high-quality lives, but on the inside they may be working very hard at stifling their true selves and desires for the sake of that security. Their actions and words have a direct connection to the flow of their money, which translates to the flow of their options and freedom.

The **9 of Pentacles (material security)** and the **5 of Swords (conflict)**, the **7 of Swords (trickery)**, the **Moon reversed (illusions to confuse)**, or the **reversed Magician (manipulation)** will signal a troubled employee or, as with a King or Queen, a vindictive partner.

The **9 of Pentacles (material security)**, **5 of Swords (conflict)**, and **Justice upright** mean a difficult court case. If Justice is reversed, it means a hard-fought battle you will most likely lose.

The **9 of Pentacles (material security)** plus the **Sun (self-expression)** means there is a benefactor to others in the public eye. Couple the above with the **Hermit card (spiritual solitude)** and you have a philanthropist who isn't in public view. They only are doing work behind the scenes and not looking for recognition.

The **9 of Pentacles (material security)** and the **Death card (end of a cycle)** plus the **King of Pentacles (financial business)** point to a trust or other type of annuity gifted to a person or business. To find out who the money would be left to, look for such things as the **10 of Pentacles (family legacy)**, the **Hierophant (religious or community centers)**, or the **Emperor (corporations)**, which could be benefiting nonprofits for causes favored by this person while living.

Be careful using the word *inheritance*, since that often triggers a fear that an elder in the family will die, and we don't predict death as advisors. Just like not being able to differentiate between just emotional affairs (fantasizing about a physical encounter) and an actual physical affair. The Death card never means that anyone stops living. It means a cycle has naturally closed and (unless the **Judgment** card is right after, which shows a **resurrection**) the cycle will not reopen. Even if Judgement is in the reading, whatever is resurrected—a business, friendship, or love relationship—will need to restart as completely new situations. On every level. The **Death** card means the end of old routines, beliefs, and assumptions.

The **9 of Pentacles (material security)** and many **Pentacle cards** around it indicate that property, land, climate, and healthcare are their preferred investment types.

46
TEN OF PENTACLES

(Family Resources)

This wonderful card represents family money and the inheritance of property and business.

This represents money and assets not earned by you, as represented in the **7 of Pentacles (personal financial growth)**. With the 7 of Pentacles, you are growing your own wealth. You are getting your own paycheck and setting money aside for your own retirement. The 10 of Pentacles represents money shared from another's efforts—a financial windfall that wasn't yours in the making but with the intent you share with younger generations.

As mentioned earlier, the word *inheritance* can be problematic, even though that one word sums up family money and material wealth handed down to younger generations. It also means family of origin (mother, father, aunt, uncle, siblings, et al.) and can be read in that context. It represents the family home along with fond memories. Early in my career, I would take notice if this 10 was reversed, I would ask my client what the family relationship was like at that moment, and every client would say it was strained or nonexistent. After thousands of readings, if this 10 is reversed, I'm comfortable assuming that the emotional health regarding the client's family ties is not positive at that moment. I would simply continue the reading with that in mind instead of bringing the topic up if it isn't a part of the specific question.

If the health of the family unit was questioned, then the Court cards in your reading will tell you which old friends or family members are the sticking points.

The **10 of Pentacles reversed (family resource)** and the **Wheel of Fortune (cycle of life)** together are clear that the current problems will heal in time. The Wheel always reminds us that happiness is cyclical. So if you're not enjoying it now, it will come back into the picture soon.

Also, the **Judgment card (resurrection)** means revisiting past misunderstandings, hurts, breakups, friends, and family for healing and grace.

The **10 of Pentacles (family resource)** and the **5 of Wands (gossip)** or the **5 of Swords (conflict/change)** will tell you there are eroding rumors with debilitating intentions putting the health of the family unit in jeopardy. It hasn't completely broken it, because the 10 is upright. But these are unwelcome cards.

To find out who is causing the problem, and for what reason, simply look for reversed Court cards for the answer. For instance:

Consider the above spread including a reversed King or Queen, which will tell you that an elder in the family is troubled and may be sabotaging the family's good emotional health. A reversed Knight, an adult. Reversed page, a child or dependent adult. As you know, each Court card has a personality of distinct likes and dislikes—explained in great detail in part 2, "Master the Court." From there you can discover the way this family got to the point that they are, and, the best part, how to get back to the center, where everyone supports each other.

PART TWO
Master the Courts

TRADITIONAL OVERVIEW OF
THE COURT CARDS

The Court cards in the Tarot represent the people in our lives. Each of the 16 cards has specific personality traits. Once you get to know and understand these distinct and interesting personalities, you will be able to describe and identify people in your clients' lives to an impressive degree.

Traditionally, the Tarot categorizes the Kings as men over 40 years old, Queens as women over 40, Knights as men and women between 18 years and 39 years old, and Pages as dependent children under 18. The suits, just like the numbered cards, have specific traits and personalities that uniquely identify them.

Many have struggled and even quit reading the Tarot because the Court cards can be difficult to understand where they fit in a reading. It's because the above rule is rigid and doesn't give room to ensure that the people in your client's life will be represented. That's why I am introducing a new way to look at each Court card that will increase your accuracy to a phenomenal degree, as it did for me when I started using this new strategy. As advisors, we combine the question asked with where a Court card lands in the throw. Here we decide if this person is contributing to a problem (reversed) or helping with a solution (upright). If the Court card appears reversed, it says to me that the card represents a person blocking a solution. Next, we describe this person to our client. Here is when it gets frustrating if you stick to the above rule of finite ages for Court families.

...

Here Are My Exceptions to These Rules
That Have Served Me Well

To start, I assess Kings and Queens as older than my client. I throw away the 40-year-old rule and read these patriarchs and matriarchs as men and women who have some sort of authority or title over my client. These people in my clients' lives are mothers and fathers or mother/father figures. They are bosses and bankers, mentors and coaches, or even best friends, if that friend has something over my client (for instance, has loaned money or knows a secret they can manipulate my client with). My client can be 55 years of age, and I do not consider a King or Queen a peer as in the traditional parameters of the Tarot. This technique makes more sense to me, and I've put it all to the test and have been a lot more accurate and concise in my readings.

I read Knights in the spread as peers, coworkers, friends, and siblings, regardless of gender and *age*. The suit traits will identify their personality, and the question asked by the client, along with the placement of the cards in the throw, will give an idea as to how they relate to your client's life.

Pages are dependent people, whether they are under 18 of age or an adult, with limited capacity to support themselves. It has been my experience that aging parents and grown children unable to leave home and live on their own are represented by the Tarot as Pages. I have discovered that often, overly *insecure or immature partners* will come through a reading as a Page as well.

"Master the Courts" goes in depth with each personality type and identifies their superpowers as well as their kryptonite. While learning the different personalities of each suit, try to align a person you know to the personality described. Once you equate, say, the Knight of Wands to your Uncle Harry, you bring all of Uncle Harry into your wisdom bank to share with your client. When you're open to it, during a well-connected reading, Spirit may place in your mind's eye the picture of a friend or relative. Trust that either their name or dominant personality traits will be pertinent to the information for your client. Reading the Court cards with this in mind will help you connect to this field of understanding, and the feedback and reviews will reflect the accuracy. So let's see which Court card your Uncle Harry fits into the best, and start creating a new and unique language with your spiritual team.

...

Master the Wands Court

Kings and Queens. I read as men and women as older than the client. Traditionally, in typical Tarot language and custom, they would represent men and women over 40 years old. Here I would like you to try a different way to look at it, since this theory works really well in my practice. It doesn't matter if your client is 20 years or 80 years old, a King is an older man and a Queen is an older woman than the person you are reading for. These could be fathers or father figures as well as mother or mother figures for the Queens. Living or dead. A King and Queen can be people who have some kind of dominion over your client, such as a boss or financial lender of any age. We read Kings and Queens as people first, but in the coming chapters I will share how I read the institution of that position more than the narrow view of a man or woman over 40 years old. You will enjoy the freedom and rich flavor this new perspective brings to your sessions.

PEOPLE AND CHARACTERS I THINK LIVE IN THE WAND FAMILY:

Beyoncé
Jeff Bezos
Justin Bieber
Greta Thunberg
Trevor Noah
Howard Stern
Stitch (Disney)
Elon Musk

Mark Zuckerberg
Elton John
Tom Cruise
Richard Branson
Inigo Montoya,
   The Princess Bride
   (1987)
Lucy Ricardo,
   I Love Lucy

Wonder Woman
Freddy Mercury
Tarzan
Bruce Lee
Daenerys Targaryen
   (Mother of Dragons),
   Game of Thrones

Wand Kings and Queens are active in every sense of the word. Work hours are put inside other hours of activities. Soccer after work or shopping on the way home. Wand adults may brag about how little sleep they need, not because they don't really need it, but because there is so much to do they can't waste time in bed. They will overbook themselves and forget to pick up something or someone off the list, mostly because they have misplaced that list. As older, possibly retired, adults, Wands will invite their adult children and grandkids into their travel plans because a constant low hum of chaos is actually enjoyable to them.

CEOs and entrepreneurs are real taskmasters and feel that being abrasive with staff will make them work harder. Nothing is further from the truth, of course, but training this out of them is difficult. Wand-controlled meetings are short and to the point. Wand admins may ask for your opinion only to shoot it down, then move on to the next person who may take the bait and suggest something as well. It's not that they don't like you or your suggestions; they just hate to waste time, even when that time involves understanding something better. They really feel if they micro-manage staff, productivity will be more efficient and people will feel better about themselves when they get so much more done.

Outside work and as love partners, they won't naturally remember birthdays and anniversaries, the biggies. They may set a reminder on their phone, but as soon as the alarm banner comes across, unless they act right away, they will most likely forget. As parents, they are interested in their children's lives but struggle with showing up at a child's soccer game, because their own workouts ran over. Older Wand parents will remain active their entire lives, and those who have made sound choices with regard to money enjoy sharing it with the family, including family in their activities and trips.

Instead of **Knights in the Wand suit** being people (men and women) in young adulthood, I feel that Knights are my client's peers, coequals, and siblings. Again, it won't matter if my client is 20 years old or 80 years old—consider a Knight to be within the same generation. The young Knight man and woman in this suit will have made incredibly fast and sometimes poor decisions in their early years. This is true in every aspect of their lives. The early years are spent jumping from focus point to focus point, unable to settle on a path of study and deciding several times during a school day that being an entrepreneur is the only way to go. They have a tough time settling into a passion because life is so awesome, fun, and distracting; they're passionate about *everything*. A service job that has an active menu would fit this young Wand idealist just fine. For instance, investing in the tools needed to wash and detail cars while corporate people are working—same with window washing or house painting where they can bid on a job, then do it on their own.

They can self-motivate and work alone quite well. Tasks that take them from place to place throughout the day are a lot more interesting than a corporate desk job. Driving jobs that serve different routes make them happy. Cooking is active and doesn't demand a high level of customer service skills, and, as mentioned earlier, Wand people really don't have the time to develop customer service skills. They are much too busy thinking about the future to worry about how they are coming across in the current moment. If they fancy themselves a life coach, they would be great at the accountability part but not so at the empathy part. To them, a goal is a goal, and not reaching it isn't an option. After all, there are 24 hours in a day, for goodness sake—plenty of time to get things done is how a Wand life coach thinks.

As young parents, they still fit in all the activities they enjoyed as single people; they just bring the kids. They aren't bothered if the children are making a scene in the café; they are unfazed by the chaos. As parents, they can be torn between supporting their children's activities and projects of their own where they can lose themselves in the process of creating. Wands change gears quickly, which comes in handy when you have little ones. They are mostly upbeat and happy, always finding it a bit hard to decide what to commit to—a project, a career, or a relationship—since they need room for choice. The feeling of freedom is so important to them, and they ask friends and family to be flexible with their "maybes" and "I might be able to fit it in" responses to invitations.

If you are married or partnered with a Wand, you may have already noticed a lack of empathy. You, as a partner, wife, husband, boyfriend, or girlfriend, may be melting down emotionally and really needing your Wand friend or family member to listen and comfort. Maybe something happened to you at work, and you could really use an attentive ear or a shoulder to cry on, but I must inform you that unless your Wand partner is very mature, you may not get the support you desire. This doesn't have to be a deal-breaker in a relationship. But the awareness that the attention span and the empathy meter just don't go very far, and this has nothing to do with how much they love you. It means they haven't the ability to put themselves in other people's shoes long enough to be a dependable source of emotional support. This is why people shouldn't have the fairy-tale idea that their partner will fulfill their every need. People who love Wands need to have a village around them, a girlfriend or guy friend they contact in case their primary Wand person is too distracted to lend support. On the other hand, if you have a problem that needs a fast *worldly, tangible* solution, Wands are your people. I'm not saying that Wands don't get animated if someone has wronged their loved one; they will get focused. But their idea of support is taking action steps. If a Wand has enough facts and a *short* list of details regarding your hardship, they will find a way to solve it. You will have no better champion. Just don't sugarcoat or beat around the bush, and for God's sake don't go into a long, drawn-out story with them. I guarantee that Wand people won't keep up with the details about feelings and will lose interest (feelings are for the Cup people). Give them the facts, the harm that was done, what will make you whole again, and they won't rest until your wholeness is reinstated.

Pages are dependent children or may show up if a parent or adult sibling is severely disabled and the person you are reading for feels an obligation to care and support. Challenging parents who want control and dominance over your grown self can show up as reversed Pages: an adult who may feel reluctantly responsible for family members and is struggling with what is expected of them. Reversed Pages can represent a person we are reading for or about acting immaturely regarding the situation.

As far as age goes, it doesn't matter if my client is 20 years old or 80; Pages are dependent people in relation to the person you are reading.

This is when you need your intuition, to figure out which scenario it represents. When I ask you to use your intuition, it's to ask Spirit for a deeper, more exact understanding of why this Page is in the lineup. You may have to ask your client if there are children involved, or a dependent adult they are responsible for emotionally or physically. Opening your mind and heart to your unique language with Spirit is what will make you a master. If you find that there are children in the family, this Page of Wands will be the active one who can't hold still. They burst into song and laughter for reasons known only to them. Time-out is torture, complete and utter torture, so be mindful of the clock or they simply won't be able to contain themselves. They are competitive and will be unbelievably sore losers (even into adulthood, they may struggle with jealousy). Here's the interesting part. It doesn't matter what the prize was that they lost. It's the sport of the game. It's always wanting to be the best. Wand children (Pages) will have a hard time concentrating, so teaching delayed gratification early in life will save you a whole lot of trouble in the coming years.

Reversed Wand Court cards. As a rule, I read Kings, Queens, and Knights as people and Pages as children or adults acting like a child. Spirit may give you an impulse to see an adult partner acting immaturely in a specific situation, but I keep that to myself and wait to see if the Page reveals him- or herself later in the reading. Reversed means everything slows down, is delayed, or that particular person isn't available to the client. Here are some examples:

In a reading about applying for a job, **Ace of Pentacles (new financial pathway)** to the **Emperor (corporations)** with a **reversed King of Wands (active, impatient, creative)** could show that the client most likely will be offered the job they interviewed for, but the reversed King shows a delay in starting. In contrast, if your client is wanting to start their **own business** (**Ace of Pentacles**) and applied for a loan (**Emperor; bank or other loan institution**), the **reversed King of Wands** would mean the loan may be delayed or not come through. (Look for the **Justice** card if you're reading about loans, since it is all about **contracts**. Upright would mean a sound promise, and reversed Justice will be a broken promise.) The rest of the cards in this reading will tell you which one it is. If the **Death card (natural endings)** shows up, most likely the position will be closed out, but your information would be kept since you are valuable to them. The reversed King doesn't show that you are not good for the job; it means that the delay or stall is internal, that something or someone within the company is slowing down the works.

In a love reading, **Two of Cups (new relationship)** with the **3 of Wands (moving well to the next level)** and **reversed Page of Wands (hyper child or delay in momentum)**. Because it's a Wand, that means action; the reverse Wand stops or slows forward momentum. This combination says the relationship (or partnership in business) is going well but needs to be slowed down to make sure everyone stays together and no one gets ahead of the other. If this Page represents a child, and your new boyfriend or girlfriend has children, it would be that an active one may be unhappy (because it's reversed) with the lack of attention they're getting. This doesn't mean the relationship will end. It gives information that allows people to make new choices for everyone involved.

Combinations I've found consistently accurate:

Reversed King or Queen of Wands will be the people who react abruptly, even explosively, to a situation, appearing immature at best. King of Wands upright is wrapped up inside their own projects, with the future of those projects locked in focus. If preoccupied with work, they have no room to think about love and vice versa. If they become impatient with someone or something (the reversed King or Queen of Wands), they will react by storming out of the room and not have a whole lot of regret about it. After all, it's just who he or she is, and there's no apologizing for what is a "natural reaction," as they see it. Upright King and Queen of Wands will react to pressure by throwing out solutions in quick and clear succession, with action steps for success. Reversed is the same King and Queen under pressure but handling it by shouting at someone, clearing the desk with one swoop of an arm, and storming out.

All reversed Court cards may represent people who aren't able to hold their peace in challenging situations. Rarely is it just that one situation provoking hurtful and poor behavior, but a buildup of many little things that may have gone wrong in the day. However, of all the suits, a reversed Wand Court card will be the most physically challenging partner in business and love. Whereas the reversed King or Queen of Swords can cut you to ribbons with their words and quick sarcasm, the suit of action (Wands) will be the most likely to punch, slap, and cause physical harm. Ask your client if they feel safe with this person when their partner or boss is angry. Even if your client says yes, just asking that question will help them emotionally separate long enough to really be an observer of the relationship in turmoil.

A LOVE READING

A woman who is struggling with the full weight and burden of the household and children, fearing divorce, asks how her estranged husband is feeling about the situation. Let's do a 10-card Celtic Cross for the answer:

Situation card—The **Hierophant (husband respects the institution of marriage)**

Crossing card—insight to what is influencing the situation, **Knight of Wands (physically moving away)**, most likely living outside the home. Which, of course, the caller has already implied with the word "estranged."

Below card, how he feels on the inside, **reversed Page of Swords (delay in communications, stubbornness and immaturity)**

Above card, what he shows on the outside, **7 of Pentacles (building a firm foundation)**—at least he is showing that on the outside; I bet he hasn't shared with anyone else the dire situation of separating from his wife.

Direct past card—past 30 days or so, what brought him to this situation—the **10 of Swords (feeling betrayed)** either by his wife or by life in general

Direct future card—next 30 days is **reversed 5 of Cups (uncertain how to handle this disappointment)**

Seventh card—how he feels about himself is **5 of Swords reversed (regretting decisions made in the moment, or the feeling of mishandling a situation)**

Eighth card—environment, which includes home as well as work, is the **6 of Wands (pride)**, proud of what he has built and doesn't want anyone to see he is going through hardships. He is missing his family.

Ninth card—hopes and fear, **Page of Wands reversed (nervous about how this situation is affecting the children)**, especially the active one, who is probably the boy or girl, who is fractious by nature and the hardest to keep behavior from fluctuating even in peace-filled times.

The final card and most probable future is reversed **9 of Swords (nearing an end of a crisis)**, bringing hope for the future.

The cards that point to recovery and reunion are nearly all of them, frankly. His worry about how this is affecting the children, as well as how this "looks" to others, is his motivator at the moment. The issue my client needs to address is his feeling of betrayal. This can be real or imagined on his part but is the heart of the issue. This information will give my client a starting place when communicating next with her husband.

CAREER QUESTION

"I went to school for engineering, but I'm finding it so boring. I need a change but don't know if I should go back to school or try something on my own."

The first part of an awesome reading is to have a firm frame of reference prior to laying down the cards. To begin, I can tell, just by the question, what kind of person my client is. He is comfortable with delayed gratification, as evidenced by his schooling, degree status, and employment in a complex occupation such as engineering. He has worked in his field long enough to grow bored, meaning that his mind is so sharp, having the ability to absorb, digest, and understand an infinite level of intricacies, and is vast. He needs life to be more stimulating, interesting, and fresh. Let's see what answers come through this Celtic Cross layout.

Situation card—**9 of Wands (ready to give up)**; this first card tells me that Spirit really understands the problem. In lots of readings, you may have an odd card where the meaning doesn't seem to fit the question. When this happens, I suggest you pass them by and read the next or even the third card, then start the reading from there. As mentioned before, I believe there are placeholder cards in a reading that need to come onto the table so the next card and position is correct. But starting this particular reading off with this card gives me confidence that there will be clear action steps coming through.

Crossing card—insight into what is influencing the situation. **Knight of Swords (impatience, single-mindedness)**. This tells me my client has a sharp mind and is successful in his communication. Should I assume he has let his manager or corporation know he is unhappy? That wasn't part of the original question, so I won't address anything about that now, because that thought that just popped into my head may not even need an answer. Let's see if the Tarot and not psychic work will answer that question. As mentioned in the last section, you will be getting a lot more information about the situation than you have time to speak of in a reading.

Below card—how he feels on the inside, **Queen of Pentacles (security-minded, generous woman)**; not sure just yet why Spirit is showing me this queen.

Above card—what he shows on the outside, **Ace of Pentacles (new financial pathway)**. This card gives the first indication that our client has shared with others, possibly his manager, his desire to start something new. If this card was the "below" card, it would tell me he was keeping his frustration with his career a secret. Just interesting to think that if he hasn't verbally shared his desire with others, it won't come as a surprise to others once he makes the change.

Direct past card—what brought him to this situation, **Page of Swords (apprehensions delays inexperience)**. I read in one-month increments, so this feeling, frustration, or challenge grew to a tipping point within the last month. And here we have it. Confirmation of the degree of seriousness he has for this topic. He is actively pursuing a solution, but his frustration and weighing out the pros and cons of creating a new direction has him sabotaging the process. This card once again speaks to how overwhelmed he must be feeling.

The first five cards of the reading tell me how he felt and what has influenced him in the last month, along with how he feels today about the question. This guy is serious about finding new work. Something that will satisfy his sharp and curious mind.

The **direct future card** is card number 6, which tells us what is synchronizing up to happen in the next month if everything stays the same. The **8 of Wands reversed (forward momentum stalls)**. If it's true we change our lives at the level of action, not at the level of wishes, it looks like our client won't, on his own, figure out some action steps to change his life. Paying for a session with me is pinning hope that I have the right combination of words to inspire and give enough confidence in him moving into action. Spirit is telling us that our client hasn't found the right connection for that spark to catch fire in a tangible way. He has plenty of desire to change. We haven't even started the reading; I'm just putting cards out and sharing my thoughts with you, in real time. I'm sure the Tarot will be offering the right combination of ideas to inspire our frustrated Page of Swords; we just haven't seen them yet.

Seventh card—how he feels about himself, **8 of Swords (feeling at no choice)**. So this combination gives us insight that he feels he can't change, because to do so would jeopardize his status and lifestyle too much. This reading is giving us x-ray vision into his personal self-talk. How we say one thing on the outside, "I can't stay in this field; I'm dying for something new," yet on the inside saying, "My work may be boring but is easy, and I have an income that affords me a lot more than if I was a student again."

Just with this combination I sense our client may feel emotionally desperate for this change in lifestyle; however, the security he will need to give up may be too high a price.

I realized, upon review, that the last assumption may sound critical of my client. I have no judgment on him but am giving you my mind chatter. The benefit of understanding my thought far outweighs the risk of someone dismissing the work because they thought I was insulting someone. That isn't my intent.

Eighth card—environment, **Lovers (partnership, union, harmony)**. Now we have a good idea about what direction Spirit is suggesting our client go in. The Lovers card is telling us he would feel safer and more hopeful if he combined resources and agreed to a business partnership of sorts. Because it is coming to us upright indicates support from family. Since the reading, however, is about career:

Ninth card—hopes and fear, **7 of Cups (fantasy/imagination/creativity)**. The card that comes up in the hopes and fears will tell us if he feels hopeful or pessimistic, and this 7 is all about being hopeful. Explained in summary.

The **final card** and most probable future **Page of Wands (curiosity driven for new things)**. Again he is interested in something new, but now we see he wants something that will be more physically active. That message keeps coming up, and, aside from the Lovers card, almost every card reflects how frustrated he feels and how insecure about going back to school or starting something brand new.

Something that happens quite a lot when you read professionally is that the initial throw just reiterates the client's frustrations and fears. This happens more than you would think. It takes bravery and boldness to make a big change in your life. To leave a relationship or a job. It takes sound risk management skills so your lifestyle and financial comfort don't shift too far from where you are at the moment.

This process of laying out the cards on the table has taken less than a minute. I know it took you a while to read through these first 10 cards in the Celtic Cross, but I put in all the thoughts that came as each card was laid down, so I implied that it took awhile.

First, I explain the way I do readings. I tell him as I lay down the cards that I am going behind his eyes to see the most probable future if his thoughts and impulses stay the same. Next, I ask if he's married or responsible for the welfare of others. The answer was yes. So now we know why the Queen is in his reading. Because he isn't alone with this decision. He says that "she doesn't care what I do; she will support me." Which is wonderful if he really believed and trusted that.

By educating the client on how manifesting works and that the Tarot can give great trajectories and confident predictions if everything stays the same, I explain, "For instance, this prediction is most probable if everything stays the same and you don't, for instance, fall back in love with your work or have such a terrible day that you quit. I continue by breaking the news that as it stands now, the next month looks like more of the same, but this spread has shined the light on things he may not be aware of.

THE READING

"The very first card out (9 of Wands) shows how you are really frustrated with your situation and ready to give up. However, even though your wife (Queen of Pentacles) says she will support you with your change, you also feel deep inside (because it is the below card placement) that financial security is very important to her. She wants you to be happy, of course, but you both have spent time building a life you love. The cards are saying the reason you feel stuck isn't so much that you don't have opportunities, because there are many places you can work as an engineer (Ace of Pentacles). It may be because you desire a more creative (7 of Cups) and active (Page of Wands) expression. You're bored, and the reason I'm not seeing you manifest the change you are looking for just might be because you don't think being bored is a good enough reason to quit." He understood what I was saying, and admitted to all of the above. He doesn't want to make his whole household suffer while he makes a big change in his life.

I told him that the card I saw in the environment placement (Lovers) points to him having a good friend he's maybe hung out with and tossed a few ideas around. Maybe because your friend is bored as well? He said he went out with a good buddy of his and talked about opening up a bar. I said, "A bar is creative and you are physically active, not to mention the people you would be with, having conversations instead of looking at a computer all day. He admitted that he was the one putting the brakes on the whole idea (8 of Wands reverse), because he was thinking he should be looking for new corporate work. The idea of a bar seemed to be growing on him.

Now that the first part of the reading opened his mind to the idea of leaving corporate work and becoming a small-business owner, the chance of getting viable information on his next steps is possible. I said, "Now that we have the awareness that you want to go into an active and creative field, let's look at the next set of cards to see how you do this."

Up until now, it looks as if the next month will feel like the previous months: a continuation of his uncomfortable feelings about what to do. To move the needle on this action, let's look forward into the future. Since the last card was a minor card, we will place more cards after that, each representing 30 days, until we get to a major card. This will give you a great idea of how long this phase will last for our client if no new action toward a new career is made.

11th card (within two months)—8 of Pentacles (focused study). "It looks like you have a pathway to study the idea. That is, if you remain open to the concept of leaving the security of a corporation in exchange for being self-employed. This card indicates you will find success and satisfaction.

12th card (within 3 months)—9 of Cups (the wish card). I read it often as the drinking or celebration card. In some decks it's even referred to as the *barkeep.* I go on to say that his course of study does indeed get him into studying a new business. I told him, I'm not saying you will actually own or purchase a bar, of course. I guess that could happen; however, my feeling is you will shadow and learn the business by being in one. By working side by side in one.

13th card (within 4 months)—Wheel of Fortune (a good-luck card). Since the last card is a Major card, this is the last card of the reading. The timeline looks like, if he chooses to pursue this dream now, he will be one more step closer to what he really wants: work he will enjoy.

I summarized this way: "We live in a world of free choice. We talk ourselves out of impulses all the time. We start saying things like I should be responsible and not make changes; however, the message is clear. If you don't choose action, and you don't get together with your buddy to talk about pulling a plan together or talk to someone who owns a bar and ask if you can't peek behind the business curtain to better understand the business, then your next few months will look a lot like the last two. Frustrating and boring. This reading does not mean you have to settle on owning a bar; it means you have to study other occupations in person to get the doors to open to you for change. You will find relief from this unsettling time, but you'll be researching what your next step would look like with various businesses.

King of Swords. Knight of Swords. Queen of Swords. Page of Swords.

Master the Swords Court
Kings and Queens

Just a reminder that I read the Kings and Queens as men and women older than the client. It doesn't matter if your client is 20 years or 80 years old; a King is an older man and a Queen is an older woman than the person you are reading for. These can be fathers or father figures as well as mothers for the Queens. Living or dead. A King and Queen can be people who have dominion over your client, such as a boss or financial lender of any age. Generally, I read Kings and Queens as people first and energy second. I would rather read the institution of that position more than the narrow view of a man or woman over 40 years old, as tradition teaches.

PEOPLE AND CHARACTERS I THINK LIVE IN THE SWORD FAMILY

Stephen King
J. K. Rowling
Albert Einstein
Nikola Tesla
Steven Spielberg
Stan Lee
Martha Stewart
Bill Gates

Sheldon Cooper,
  The Big Bang Theory
Miranda Priestly,
  *The Devil Wears
  Prada (2006)*
Judge Judy
Tony Stark, *Iron Man*
Jessica Fletcher,
  Murder, She Wrote

Spock, *Star Trek*
Hermione Granger,
  Harry Potter
Lisa Simpson,
  The Simpsons
Amy Farrah Fowler,
  The Big Bang Theory
Rob Reiner, *director*

Sword people are in pursuit of perfection. They think and puzzle over the best strategies and seek a ton of data before moving forward on a project. If you have a proposal for a Sword person, please have your backup sources available or they won't take your idea seriously. They are vigilant about what is going on around them, rarely missing or dismissing someone's tardiness or minor mistake. Swords will look at a piece of work someone delivered, and have an overwhelming impulse to add their red pencil marks. A mature member of the Sword family will have some restraint over this irritating habit, since they have discovered, over the many years of marking up other people's work, that action has a habit of eroding a person's self-esteem and feeling of worth. The mature Kings and Queens of this suit will be less inclined to lean into their natural tendency, of being overtly critical of others. Does this mean more experienced and mature Sword people don't notice the errors? Not at all, but they have learned to let some things pass for their own mental health.

Swords are famous for order. Labels and clear filing systems both at work and at home. You most likely will see a calendar displaying a minute-by-minute structure well into the year. A pantry that is so neat that they put its beauty and perfection to show it off, with the intent of inspiring the rest of us.

Kings and Queens as CEOs notice holes in the staff's fabric of production. He or she notices risk and will manage that information conservatively. If in your reading you have a King or Queen of Swords and you assess that that card represents the client's person of interest, understand that part of the problem this couple may be having is the critical and pessimistic nature of their Sword partner. They aren't as stubborn as, say, a Pentacle family member, but the Sword person still has the need for facts and figures to change their minds about something. Their general pessimism will make it unlikely you will be able to move them unless your facts are clear and presented concisely. They don't know they are as critical as they come across to others. The secret to dealing with your critical Sword husband, wife, or boss is to be lighthearted about whatever new idea you want to discuss. Saying things like, "Hello there; I just want you to know that I will be presenting a new idea soon. I will give you a quick overview now so you can say no right away and get that over with. After that, I will bring in the facts and figures I've gathered that lead me to believe it's a great idea."

A Sword person won't normally boast or interrupt a conversation, volunteering all they know on a topic. A team at work can openly be struggling with a problem and, unless a Sword member in the office *is invited* into the meeting *and asked* for their opinion, they won't offer solutions. If asked, however, their thoughts on the problem, they provide instant, viable resolutions. According to them, their perspective and opinion will be the most accurate and well researched. And it's been my experience that they most likely will be absolutely correct on that assumption.

Sword Kings and Queens (older than the client) with children and grandkids will provide educational activities during family gatherings. Museums, holidays to ancient ruins, or trips to all the dams in the US are some of their favorites.

Knight of Swords (a client's contemporary) as parents are curiosity driven, orderly, and cautious. They consume information as if they will be teaching it, because after all, they enjoy lecturing to anyone who may ask a question. Family road trips to national parks and cities rich with history would be a pleasure for any Sword adult to give to the younger ones. As parents, they have menus created for the week or month and a place for the kids to hang their coats and store their shoes, with a routine that rarely wavers. Swords don't cut corners, and they read every word in a user's manual. If you suggest they skip over a few paragraphs, the Sword person will stare at you like you've lost your mind.

Regarding occupations, think of all that have a list of rules to follow. With legal occupations, where facts have a history of being black and white, Swords are free to monitor the well-defined boundaries. Jobs that have very little gray area, one with a more nuanced set of mandates, will feel much more comfortable for our Sword people. Careers in law enforcement and the military suit Sword people well. The Wand person leans into the exciting and spontaneous showmanship occupations; the Swords are all about order and accountability. Engineering, science, and teaching are comfortable ways of making a living for them.

Does anyone you know come to mind with this description? Maybe a boss or sibling? If you are able to identify someone with these traits, bring all of that person's variables that you know on a personal basis into the reading. Understand that the person you are labeling with that particular Court card will bring you added information about the questions at hand. You don't need to know someone personally to add them to the various archetypes in the Tarot. If a close friend, coworker, or family member doesn't come to mind, then a character on your favorite TV show will do. As a matter of fact, I've labeled the Page of Swords as the character Sheldon Cooper from *The Big Bang Theory* sitcom. And yes, Pages are supposed to be dependent children or disabled adults, but the Sheldon Cooper *character* reflects the way I read the Page of Swords. Always slowing down the conversation, needing to clarify the facts as it progresses. Worrying about the future to the point of trying to control the present, in the hope of avoiding unnecessary discomfort. Like having to sit in a certain spot, having a tidy room, and needing emotional assistance when things don't go his way. Oh yes, a young Sword can test you to tears as they closely watch and critique your driving and remind you if schedules start straying too far off what they expect to happen. These wonderful, smart, and quick-witted kids can be inflexible in negotiations and, if pushed, can risk an emotional meltdown, stalling any momentum a parent has managed to establish.

I have discovered that the **reversed Page of Swords (delay)** is quite trouble-some, and rarely can a family member talk them out of slowing up the whole process. Whatever that process might be. Here are some of the combinations and reversals that pop up most often in my readings:

Reversed Justice (broken contracts) combined with **reversed Page of Swords (delay in communications, stubbornness, and immaturity)** means that agreements on all topics may need to change. If there is an agreement or a "contract" that a child will finish schoolwork at a certain time, the reversed Justice indicates that there will most likely be resistance to authority. If the reading is about money or adult matters, the warning is the same: to be prepared for plans to change. Because the Justice card (a Major card) is present, this indicates that the client is assuming something that is set in stone. Cautioning them to be emotionally flexible around the topic at hand will ensure a more casual reaction if the news of a delay comes in. There is a unique combination that has always been correct in a love reading, and it is when I see the **3 of Wands (looking from a distance)**. I ask my client if they are in a long-distance relationship, and if the answer is yes and I see any **Sword card (thoughts/thinking)**, then the following cards will tell me how her long-distance lover is feeling about the situation: if he is leaning into the relation-ship or away from it. The Sword card coming in after this 3 indicates the partner is thinking but, more accurately, is *over*thinking the situation about loving someone far away. The Sword card will point more toward pessimism than optimism at this point. If the next card is the **Ace of Wands (beginning new actions)** with the **8 of Wands (fast energy, possibly travel)**, it would be best for the success of the rela-tionship that your person of interest meets your client face to face soon to anchor the relationship. This may not be a conscious thought for your long-distance lover at the time of the reading. Giving your client this information means they can preemptively suggest meeting in person and offset or completely avoid his or her feelings of pessimism about the relationship being successful. Forewarned is fore-armed. This is how a person can influence a credible trajectory and mold a more preferable future with a new action.

Reversed 4 of Swords (introspective rest and recovery) with the **reversed Knight of Swords (chaotic situation)**. This combination gives me the impression that my client is choosing not to take breaks, even though breaks from the chaos are available (4 of Swords). This is a good point to bring up by saying something like, "I see here that there are things you resist delegating to people because you feel you need control over the situation. This absolutely speaks to a person's need to control. But they come by it innocently, because human nature dictates that if we feel we are losing control over the party, project, or relationship, we hold on tighter to, it is hoped, navigate things to quieter days. But the **4 of Swords (rest and recovery)** needs to be addressed and encouraged for the client to have the proper perspective to succeed. I know I've mentioned this before, but it's been my experience that the **4 of Swords upright (rest and recovery)** literally means that self-care is necessary and available, but the 4 of Swords *reversed* doesn't mean there isn't rest and recovery available. It indicates a missed or soon-to-be-missed opportunity to take a break.

I've had several conversations with divorcing parents who want to know how the next step in their divorce will go. After answering that one question and I see a **reverse Page (of any suit)**, I ask if they have children. If the answer is yes, even if it is more than one child, I will talk about the one who has the same traits as that suit. Reversed Pages show that a young one is having trouble with the process. In particular, a **reversed Page of Swords (delay, frustration)**. This child wants to slow everything down by causing enough trouble that the focus moves off the divorce and onto him or her. They are bright and curious children but can really put a stop to things with their emotional breakdowns. The antidote for this is to have one-on-one conversations about what is happening with the family, and reassure them they are safe and loved. Swords need communication, so to the best of your ability and with respect for their age, of course, talk to them so they won't feel the need to act out.

Just had an interesting text reading. Stephanie writes, "Can you please tell me what intentions Scott has in mind for our relationship?" I write back that I would be happy to answer that, but a frame of reference is needed. I asked if they were exclusive or casually dating. She answered, "We have been seeing each other for two years now, but he has not named it yet." I told her I was sorry he was being so lazy about the relationship, but was happy to look into how he is thinking from his point of view.

First card: **Hermit (quiet reflection) crossed** with the **reversed Page of Swords (delay)**. Next card: **King of Pentacles (very slow-moving, methodical)** into the **9 of Swords (losing sleep over the situation)** to the **reversed Knight of Wands (not moving forward)**. I write, "I see he isn't sharing any of his thoughts (Hermit), but he is definitely in a delay mentality over this relationship (reversed Page of Swords). He does worry about losing you (9 of Swords) but doesn't want to move forward into a committed relationship, especially one toward marriage, not even to move in with each other (reversed Knight of Wands), and I'm not sure why, so let me look farther ahead" (the future cards show everyday life for him). I have some Pentacles and some Wands showing everyday money and activities, but nothing new about the relationship. I told her that my readings go out several months, not years, and I can see that the next couple of months will be much like the last couple of months, which answers your original question, as heartbreaking as it sounds." I then remind her that this is his reading, meaning that if left on his own, without outside influence, he won't have the impulses to improve the relationship and bring you more security. Something I noted but didn't say was that Scott had **Death (natural ending)** and the **7 of Wands (defending his position)**, but I still couldn't see why that after two years he'd gotten to this point. Until I could understand it, I wasn't going to mention anything. I then said, "Let me see if there is anything you can do at the level of action to influence and, it's hoped, change this trajectory." The next several cards tell me everything; more specifically, the last card shows the overall energy: the **reversed Queen of Swords (defensive and argumentative)**. This is an example of Spirit telling me more information *about my client* so I can better understand why Scott is not progressing. The situation has become very difficult for Stephanie because she is trying to control and convince Scott to be more committed. The reversed Queen of Swords shows a woman who has lost her patience and can be direct, sarcastic, and overly reactive, bringing out a defensiveness in Scott (7 of Wands). No one is born a reversed Queen (or King) of Swords; we grow into one. Overwhelmed by not getting our needs met and remaining available to someone who isn't respecting our time erodes our self-esteem and eats away hope for a better future. "Stephanie," I said, "It's wise, especially in the beginning of a relationship, to give to someone only what they are giving you, so resentment doesn't build up. And as hard as this may be to hear, I suspect you have already started to bring your heart back from him. He is mishandling the love, attention, and availability you have given him. Allowing him to hold your heart in his hands is a very dangerous thing to do. You know you have done that when his actions (or inactions, in this case) cause a negative emotional consequence. A deep feeling of uncertainty when communications go quiet for a day or two affects your outlook, your mood, your work productivity, and your normally peaceful heart. Bring your heart back, and love through your head and not your emotions to be able to evaluate if Scott is a practice boyfriend or a proper one. He needs to earn your attention, not assume your availability."

I never told Stephanie about the reversed Queen of Swords being in her reading. That would come off as accusatory. An uncaring advisor may read it as "Well, if you weren't so defensive and demanding, he wouldn't have left in the first place," but how supportive would that be? As mentioned earlier, no one is born a reversed King or Queen; life sort of molds us into one when our hopes for a certain outcome start looking like something uncertain. We panic and start compulsively planning how we will pull the train back onto the track by using our brute strength and grit.

The takeaway from this chapter is remembering that Swords indicate a sharp mind that's curiosity driven, quick thinking, and so educated that not finding a solution to a problem is rare. The shadow side is when activities outside our control compel us to overthink and overanalyze, and a negative-thinking loop occupies every waking moment. Enjoyable occasions and casual camaraderie are a chore because your mind has found some sort of odd comfort in mulling over a problem to discover a new idea you could offer that will give way to a solution you would be happier with.

Master the Cups Court

The fun-loving, emotionally driven and inspired Cup family consists of people you can always pick out of a crowd. At a movie, they will be the ones ugly crying or overheard teaching a child about kindness and tolerance. They believe that intuition is based on how you feel about a topic, when that couldn't be further from the truth. Thinking something must be true because you feel it deep in your soul to be true means real-world decisions being made by emotions. More often than not, heavy real-world consequences arrive in short order.

PEOPLE AND CHARACTERS I THINK LIVE IN THE CUPS FAMILY

Oprah Winfrey
Tom Hanks
Keanu Reeves
Ryan Gosling
Sebastian, *The Little Mermaid (Disney)*
Tyler Perry
Walt Disney
Bob Ross

Ken Jeong, comedian— Russell in the movie *Up (2009)*
Peter Quill, *Guardians of the Galaxy (2014)*
Hagrid, *Harry Potter*
Jack Dawson, *Titanic (1999)*
Robin Williams
Carol Burnett

Willy Wonka, *Willy Wonka & the Chocolate Factory (1971)*
Phoebe Buffay, *Friends*
Michael Scott, *The Office*
Genie, *Aladdin* (Disney)
Dory, *Finding Nemo*
Mister Rogers
Fezzik, *The Princess Bride*

Yes, Cup people do have intuitive abilities like the rest of us, but the difference is that when the information from the upper octaves is filtered through a person's emotions, they can't be sure of what is real and what is simply them feeling a certain way. For the most part, I've understood and experienced intuitive information coming through in factual ways. If I feel an impulse of emotion during a reading, then I know I am no longer using my intuition but reading through my imagination, where emotions live. Many successful advisors do their intuitive work by this method, and they are called empaths. Their jobs can be very taxing since, after a day of work, their emotions have gone through so many ups and downs that they are exhausted.

Running your life by the way you feel means life's pulling you around by the seat of your pants. Not being aware of this means being emotionally affected by the world around you, which is exhausting. A member of the Cup family who hasn't discovered the nuances of a sensitive heart may be driving around feeling great until she or he witnesses what they believe to be a troubling event. A homeless man with a skinny dog can lead to a deep emotional reaction or something on the outside triggering a not-so-nice memory that, if left unchecked or consciously managed, devolves a good mood into the ground.

Cup people have beautiful hearts and caring souls that bring meaning to our lives, sometimes at a high cost to their own, since they are constantly mirroring back our best selves. They kindly remind us to write thank-you cards and not to talk badly about others. They are the first to take your coat, offer tea, and point to the most comfortable chair, encouraging that we be comfortable. They look you in the eye and are truly interested in knowing how you're doing and feeling. They are genuinely interested in your well-being and emotional health.

Our wise Queens, Kings, and Knights of Cups have learned to protect their own mental and emotional health by navigating away from compulsively negative people and situations. Maturity has its benefits, as one has learned the hard way, meaning that spending a lot of time trapped in other people's dramas really bums them out. They've discovered through the years which people deserve their light heart and loving nature and who will just take a Cup person's time and effort without putting in any new action to make positive change.

Let me introduce you to an emotionally balanced Cup person. They hold our attention with their optimism. Amazing storytellers and writers make it seem as if they were born with a deep understanding of the human condition, and listening to them educates and inspires. The mature King and Queen of Cups have unshakable positivity; the glass is always half full. They have a unique ability to connect with everyone they meet by putting everyone at ease. If a mature Cup person sincerely likes you, they will, without question, like your friends as well. They love to laugh and are cheerful by nature. As event planners, you can be sure there will be more than enough food, entertainment, and music. All vendors will be paid in full and tipped well, since they understand the struggle of everyday life. Thinking they were the cause of anyone's hardship or uncertainty would devastate them. They just couldn't live with themselves without making it right as soon as the unintentional mistake was realized.

It would be much easier for them to be in supportive fields such as HR positions, if they look to work in the corporate world, than they would feel to be the boss. As beautiful as their hearts are, a staff member's sad story will move them every single time. Hard boundaries are not their strong suit. Occupations in the beauty and health industries as well as being responsible for the success of happy events are more in line with a healthy Cup person. They can be successful in their own business when the focus is on the well-being of other people. Members of the Cup family succeed as therapists of all kinds, as life coaches, and in fields that care for children and animals. In fact, if they are politically minded, they will advocate for children and animals very effectively. Between their storytelling skills and the ability to move people to action with their sincerity and undying devotion to what is good and right, there will never be a lost soul without a loving home. Every nonprofit should look for a member of the Cup family to run the show for them. They will mirror back your best self, and as long as you occasionally return the favor, you will have no better champion for your cause.

Cup people will send and receive the most holiday cards. Why? Because holidays are the perfect canvas for Cups to create on: create parties and gatherings big and small. It's all about celebrating life and love. They will be the ones with the most friends on Facebook and the most people in their contacts. They have friends everywhere and can keep in touch with everyone. They strive to be inspiring, flexible, and optimistic.

Even though I mentioned earlier that Kings, Queens, and Knights of Cups find it emotionally challenging being the CEO of a structured company, you will be impressed by their ability to present at a meeting. There are no better motivators than Cup people. Their ability to make everything sound simple is a real gift. If your business has a problem and you need someone to motivate staff to devote more time to the solutions, then hire this member of the Court to lead the project. Your staff will be so inspired by the presentation that the turnaround will be nearly instant.

Unlike Sword people, who never volunteer solutions unless they are formally asked, Cups will spew out options just by walking down the hall and overhearing a conversation. Their ideas don't follow a set pattern by conventional means. They are able to brilliantly twist and turn situations into new shapes, therefore guaranteeing new solutions. Coworkers (or their kids, if we are talking about their private life) may look annoyed at each other and roll their eyes at Cup's suggestions, but I promise, every single thing that Cup people propose is quietly considered by others and oftentimes picked up and used. And there's the rub. Not often will others give Cup coworkers credit for the idea. "But why should we?" they protest. "It was offered so carefree and generously like it was a gift," they say, justifying it and claiming the idea as their own. A business runs the risk of losing this valuable member of the team if credit is withheld too often. That being said, it is easy to celebrate and honor a Cup person. They don't need much, but don't mistake a generous nature for weakness. They won't stay and fight with the person who took their idea as their own; they will, however, quietly leave and settle into a new place that returns to them what they give to others: respect, inspiration, a healthy dose of optimism, and their ability to inflate confidence in others.

As parents, Cup people may be overly concerned with how their family feels about things, and takes it personally if others are upset. The shadow side of Cups' personality lives in the belief that they are somehow responsible for the emotional happiness or sadness of others. Cups are true empaths and are able to energetically and emotionally meet a person where they are and guide them to happier moods; well, that's the positive side. They can also annoy the heck out of you when they helicopter, hovering around their children or troubled friend, reciting what I call spiritual bumper sticker slogans such as "This too will pass" and "The universe has your back," denying that person the grace allotted to everyone in a rotten mood. If all of their first efforts to move you to a happy place fail, they will lose patience and step away, though they don't give up easily. Allow them to stay and Cup people will happily talk you into lighter feelings. A person just can't take all that goodness and stay bummed out. If the person your friendly Cup is trying to uplift doesn't move into a happy mood, it would be in our Cup person's best interest that they leave the crabby friend with their despair before it rubs off on them. Being an empath does have its downsides, since the moods of others stick to this emotionally absorbent soul.

Page of Cups (sensitive child) is the one to emotionally collapse in a heap on the floor if things don't go their way. They become deeply disturbed by violence and cruelty of any kind. Gory horror shows will guarantee nightmares, since their fragile psyches just can't process the display of pain and fear depicted in the show. If the **reversed Page of Cups** is present, then the **child is struggling** with the situation the client has asked about, and may not know how to tell you. The only thing your client may notice is bad behavior for no apparent reason. Trust me, there is always a reason, but he or she is just a child feeling things more deeply than the rest of the family and feeling alone with the sadness. A little one-on-one time, along with an extra dose of loving messages, will improve their sense of security and trust.

When doing readings, my frame of reference is always the four corners of the question at the start. The throw will be a snapshot of what's going on right at the moment. If there are reversed Courts anywhere in the lineup, they will be the people in the family having the most trouble. I ask Spirit to show me the blocks and restrictions that are present at the moment that might be keeping my client from their happiness and desired goals. After discovering all that is understood about the present moment, laying down more cards reveals the most likely scenario if nothing changes in the client's thinking or choices. If the most probable future isn't to the client's liking, then simply changing perspectives or pathways to that goal is all you need for success. Remember to reframe the question out loud as you go and not just in your head, or else the information you give won't be easily understood by the client.

MEDIUMSHIP EXAMPLE

When doing a regular reading, any reversed Court card will represent a person who may be a block or restriction in regard to the question at hand—in the perspective of living people, and day-to-day life in general. If you are doing mediumship, know that I read any reversed Court as a deceased person, and every upright Court as a person still living. The way I do this is simple, and you may like this technique. If you are starting the reading *with the intention of mediumship*, the reading or messages from that passed loved one do not begin until the next card *after* your first reversed Court card. The reading starts from there. Often a few reversed cards will show up in a row, signaling that the passed loved one is with other passed family members. Remember that the personality traits of the suit will give you enough information for a good description that your client will be able to identify the particular loved one. Some gifted advisors with honed psychic skills may get names and finite details. The message for the client begins right after the reversed Court card. There may be only a few cards before you feel the message has finished. If perhaps you have a reversed Court card, indicating a passed loved one coming through, and right after an upright Court card, then the passed loved one is asking you to deliver the message to someone else who is still alive.

How this spread looks on the table and how you deliver the messages means you start with the intention of mediumship. Put one card after the other, upright in a pile, until you get a reversed Court; let's say it's the reversed Queen of Cups. Remembering that all the Kings and Queens are older than the client (even if your client is 80 years old), you would describe this woman as someone who was a mother or mother figure, or a grandmother. Then start describing this person with the suit traits. "She was kind and generous and tried hard to be attentive and have time for you." Most likely a familiar personality will dawn on your client; if not, just carry on with the reading, saying, "It's all right if no one comes to mind; I'll give the message and you can put it in your pocket for later." If another Court card right after that appears in the upright position, then you describe to your client the personality of that Court member, adding that the following message is for your client to deliver to that particular person. If there isn't an upright Court card next to the reversed one, then the message is for your client. Here are some thoughts about how that would go.

The next card down after the reversed Court starts the reading. From many years of readings, I have noted that if the next card is a 5 from any suit, it indicates conflict either inside the family or inside your client's heart. Here are some examples:

Next to the reversed Court comes the 5 of Cups (guilt and remorse). The message you give is "She sees you are way too hard on yourself. Her message is to please don't have any guilt around my passing." If the 10 of Pentacles (inheritance, legacy) appears, followed by a 5 in any suit, it means as follows. The 5 of Cups: "Please do what you want with what I left, and thank you for all you've done for me; don't feel guilty about anything. All is well." The 5 of Swords: "I see conflict in your thinking regarding what is left behind. I know this is a challenging time, but try to have troubled thoughts pass through you." The 5 of Wands (remember, these are cards that are following the 10 of Pentacles and talking about the tangibles left behind for others): "There seem to be arguments either on the outside of you with other family members or within yourself. Please know all will be settled in time." This one can also be an "I'm sorry for not setting up my final wishes clearly enough to avoid this conflict." The 5 of Pentacles: "I'm sorry you feel left out, or that there should be more. Trust me when I say I will be working behind the scenes on your behalf regarding your financial security."

When doing mediumship, the messages are always uplifting and positive. Learn to hear the other side, and you will bring about healing for your client and other family members.

Back to regular readings while working with members of the Cup Court. When a Court card of this suit appears reversed, it means there's an internal struggle with the topic. I receive a lot of love questions, and if the **Knight of Cups (messages of love)** shows up reversed, I've discovered it doesn't mean the exact opposite (that their POI is not in love with them but, rather, isn't interested in showing love to them). The surrounding cards will tell you why. If perhaps the **10 of Swords (feeling betrayed)** speaks to either the present or the future (depending on position), they are fearful of falling in love with someone and being hurt like in their past relationship. They say they are afraid of commitment because they are afraid of getting hurt. If ever a potential partner says this the first time, remind them that just because it happened in the past doesn't mean that this will be their experience now. If they bring it up more than once, there is a problem, since it is code for *"Get over this idea of a future with me."* They are using this reason *not* to create a healthy progressive relationship with you. We've all been hurt by loving someone who didn't love us back or fell out of love with us. Using it as a reason to withhold a happy future is shortsighted and hurtful to anyone who would like to share a life with them. *If* he or she is not saying it out loud. You will be able to see a passive-aggressive way of communication with the **5 of Swords (damaging chances for success)** or the **7 of Swords (creating illusion and manipulation)**. It's human nature to hold back and not make big declarations until you're sure about your feelings. But not talking to your partner about your anxieties makes you appear selfish and hurtful.

Most often, this combination tells me that this POI is letting his or her actions of not replying to texts and emails say they aren't interested in a deeper relationship.

KING of PENTACLES.

NIGHT of PENTAC

QUEEN of PENTACLES.

PAGE of PENTACLES.

Master the Pentacles Court

By this part of the book, you have probably caught on how much I love to explore each suit's personality. The information I'm sharing with you has helped me so much in my work. I hope while you have been reading each description that people in your life come to mind—that one of the descriptions reminded you of a family member or friend when obsessed with a project. Thinking, "Oh, that reminds me of my uncle when he's focused on something." So when that particular Court card shows up in a reading, and depending on the question at hand, you have *Uncle's character traits*, including habits and hobbies, pop into your mind. You will then do your reading from that awareness. As mentioned earlier, you can also assign a famous figure and describe their attributes, quirks, and successes to the client. The King of Pentacles brings President Jimmy Carter to mind. He is a quiet seeker and what I call an Earther, meaning someone who values nature, since he was a peanut farmer in his early life. He also has a deep feeling of responsibility for the human condition, as exhibited by his dedication to Habitat for Humanity. These universal Earthers rejuvenate in nature, and most enjoy gardens, both flowers to create natural beauty and food to share with friends, family, and neighbors. Another person who comes to mind for me when working with the Pentacle Court family is chef Jose Andres, since he travels to places suffering from natural disasters and while there he helps feed everyone. Also, the entire medical profession belongs to the Pentacle family.

Each Court card can give so much information over and beyond just traits. If Spirit has directed your awareness to someone you know, there is a good reason. Either that person's name is important (especially if doing mediumship) or something that stands out about them will be significant and will bring added value to the conversation. I have applied many identities and people's personalities to my Court cards, and Spirit never fails to point my attention to someone in my life who resembles the person or situation that is discussed.

Before diving into our Pentacle family, I want to clarify one thing—even though a bit off topic. When doing mediumship, you may have a friend, celebrity, or family member pop into your mind without the prompting of a reversed Court card. Instead of pushing the thought away, consider the name of that person being valuable to the conversation. One time, my neighbor Cindy came to mind during a reading, and I asked the client if the name Cindy meant anything to them, and it did; it was the name of the diseased loved one. If this happens to you and the answer is yes, continue describing your friend's personality, accomplishments, and virtues and apply it to the reading. If the answer is no, suggest your client make a note of it, and maybe it will become relevant later in the session. This is the way you build a unique language between you and your spirit guides. When you start trusting that language, you start making a difference in people's lives.

IT'S TIME TO DIVE INTO OUR PENTACLE FAMILY

The Pentacle suit has the slowest energy or feeling in the deck. Every suit has its own momentum. The Wands, Swords, and Cups are all action, thought, and emotion. Nothing that walks on the earth. Pentacles are the tangibles in life—in other words, what you can hold in your hands. When doing a reading with a lot of Pentacles, your timelines need to be a bit slower. I like to work in one-month increments as a rule, but if I have a reading heavy in this suit, I will extend the amount of time it may take for a client to reach their goal or get the job or date.

PEOPLE AND CHARACTERS I THINK LIVE IN
THE PENTACLES FAMILY

Jimmy Carter

Michael Bloomberg

Jane Goodall

Sean Penn

Alexi Navalny

Jose Andres, chef

Pope Francis

Anthony Fauci

Julia Child

Archie Bunker,
  All in the Family

Blanche Devereaux,
  The Golden Girls

Peter Thiel, PayPal

Woody, *Toy Story*

C. Montgomery Burns,
  The Simpsons (1989)

Mr. Miyagi,
  The Karate Kid

Warren Buffett

Desmond Tutu

In the workplace, a Pentacle staff member or management will be slow to change direction. Wand employees are quick and have a hard time listening to an entire message before protesting against it. Swords will take the idea offered and start the spreadsheets and data points. Cup people will craft and mold the message as optimistic and uplifting. Pentacles counterbalance them all and will be stone quiet in the meeting, without expression. They will take the meeting in stride, not having an opinion pro or con, go back to their desks, and start building their day around the way they were directed. If they did have an opinion, it would probably lean toward the negative.

They will not be late for any commitment, since their word is their bond. Once they find a career that provides the level of income they desire, they will stay with it. Doesn't matter if they enjoy it—they don't need to be entertained at their jobs; as long as the monetary benefits meet their level of comfort, you can count on them showing up and getting things done. The only caveat to this is if a Pentacle person is asked to do or say anything against their moral and ethical standards. That is their red line no one should cross.

Living their lives entirely fact based makes them highly sought after in financial and securities fields. They are good at running their own business; however, you most likely won't find them in a startup without it being thoroughly vetted. The risk level is too high. They are extremely careful with money. The businesses you will find Pentacle people owning are real estate, property management, securities, and established franchises—tried-and-true business models, so they can retain their calm and methodical way of living their lives.

In corporate life, they prefer to work behind the scenes as far away from the brainstorming marketing team down the hall as possible. All that enthusiastic shouting and laughing as they fill their whiteboards to capacity is not their happy place. Drama of any kind, at their job or at home, is avoided at all cost.

They can gossip; don't get me wrong. Pentacle people have opinions and impulses to talk about someone's choice of clothes or goals, and those opinions slant toward negativity. Even though the one card in the deck that actually means *gossip* is in the Wand suit (the 5 of Wands), Pentacle people relish in mumbling to others in passing little bits of skepticism about something.

Depression doesn't visit often, but when it does, what helps them out of it will be diving into a project for days. If they are upset or around confusing emotions set off by others, the task they choose will not be to solve the emotional situation. Pentacle people know that emotions are transient and will pass. If their partner in love or business is overtly upset, they will patiently listen; then, after the animated person falls in a heap on the floor, exhausted from the explanation, Pentacles will retreat to work on something that has four edges, such as mowing the lawn, tending to the car, cleaning house, or fixing the lamp that's been awaiting repair for months. What better time to get to that *to-do list* but now, when people are hard to understand due to all that messy emotion? They will do anything except sit down and talk with someone in a fractious state of mind. They will wait until calm reenters and a quiet conversation returns, as long as it's sober and logical.

Pentacle people love deeply, and it doesn't matter if they are older, a King, a Queen, or just starting out as Knights; most will be traditionally minded and long to be married and raise a family. Building wealth for the people they love is paramount. Money equals options, and the main goal is to provide those options to the ones they love.

Pentacles are excellent listeners but have a hard time dealing with displays of deep emotion, especially anger and tears. They value family and home over anything else and will fight for its health and survival. The Pentacle family's solutions are pragmatic and orderly.

They are the ones to stay in a challenging marriage because of the children and the legacy. That being said, even though people in this Court are not competitive, if the partner of a Pentacle wife or husband insists on divorce, you will have a hard time separating this Pentacle from their money, investments, and family time. They purchase only the best, with legacy in mind. If items break, they will find a way to fix them, so as not to waste time, effort, and resources purchasing new if they can avoid it. When balanced, this Court family won't pester others. Even Pages (children) are pretty easygoing and friendly. If you ask a Pentacle Page to do a task, say, empty the garbage, they will find a discreet way of asking, "What's in it for me?" If they are given allowance, they are careful with it and don't spend frivolously. Pentacle children do what they're supposed to do. They follow the rules and, for the most part, take on their missions without protest, since they tend to be quiet observers instead of dramatic protesters.

When doing a reading and these calm, easygoing people show up, you now know them better. A combination and reversal I've found interesting and reliably accurate is this:

King or Knight of Pentacles in a love reading (**quiet stable people**) and the **reversed King, Queen, or Knight of Swords (augmentative)**. In this particular combination, where the low-key Pentacle person is put into a position to endure an angry Sword person, our Pentacle pal will sit quietly during the dramatic rage. And boy, can a Sword person rage; for the most part, it is on a verbal level. I can be sure and comfortably trust that the Pentacle person, during this fight, will be making plans to move out of the relationship. Pentacle people are slow to establish relationships and *quiet* to leave one. They will do and say anything it takes to stop the madness, and perform the same way days after the incident, but make no mistake: they are planning their escape. It will not be a rash decision, but when the decision is made, they will leave the relationship completely with steadfast determination.

Any reversed Court card will represent a person's shadow or dark side, but I've found the Sword Court to be the most destructive emotionally and the Wand Court physically. When Wand people are provoked, there is little time between thought and action, but it's been my experience that action is leaving the room *before* they get physical with their partner. Reversed Cup people will simply go into themselves, not harming anyone but themselves with deep grief about the situation.

HOW TO USE COURT CARDS AS SIGNIFICATORS

Something fun to try when learning the Courts is to do this type of relationship reading. A significator is when you choose one Court card to represent each of the people you're reading. It's a Court card you choose and keep separate from the deck that represents the client and the client's person of interest. After being chosen, the card is placed on the table, and the information received during the reading is filtered through this person's traits and views, leading the way for a very comprehensive and enlightening session.

You don't need to find a couple in love for this; it can be anyone from siblings to business coworkers or just friends. Any two people who would like to know how the other feels about the relationship in general or how the other is feeling after, say, an argument or collaborative project. Most readers find a Court card that best represents each person's personality; however, when reading strangers, you don't want to quiz your client about what their significant other is like; after all, you're a psychic, right?

Allow Spirit to reveal what persona each person desires to show, by shuffling the deck and finding the first two Kings or Queens that present themselves.

It's best to use two separate decks when doing this kind of partnership reading, since many times the same card will turn up in the same position, showing where the couple agrees. I use only Kings representing males and Queens representing females as significators. If reading for same-sex couples, use two Queens or Kings. When laying the cards down, it doesn't matter if they are reversed, since that doesn't have any meaning with this particular type of reading. Remember, in a regular psychic reading a reversed Court card reveals a person who is a block or restriction for the client. And in a mediumship reading, all reversed Court cards represent deceased people, and upright cards represent living people. For this reading, we simply want the first King or Queen of any suit upright or reversed to act as a representative of the client and the person they are asking about. When working with one deck, once a King or Queen shows up, leave that card down and replace all other cards back into the deck and reshuffle.

As far as a spread, there are many to choose from. If the situation is dire or extreme, such as a couple had a fight, or one has a goal the other doesn't support and the client wants to know why, I use the Celtic Cross spread. It will show a timeline as to when things may have started to heat up and cause a sticking point. You will be delightfully impressed by how much information this approach will reveal.

When doing this reading in person with both people present, using two decks by the same creator that have the same images is really impressive for the clients. The visual of having the same card show up at the same point just blows people away. It can be the same card in the same position, saying that both parties are on the same page regarding the question, or when the opposite cards land in the same position, showing the problem area. But what if both readings have completely different cards showing up? Well, that says there is no common ground or interest in the other person's goals. Not to blame anyone; it's simply valuable information that shines light on where and how to start the conversation.

PART THREE
Master the Majors

DECODING THE MAJOR ARCANA

DIVINE COUNCILS

The Major Arcana or mysteries asks the advisor to back up far enough from the situation at hand to see the perfection in it. By doing this, you will discover a deeper understanding leading to a deeper peace. To understand what the Major cards are trying to communicate, I would like to share my understanding of **Guardians, Teachers/Mentors, Guides, and Angels**. Studying many sources on my way to understanding the messages over my lifetime, I approach the Major Arcana from the following perspectives. If something feels right to you, take it, and do your readings from that understanding. Toss aside anything you don't align with.

Reading the Major cards pulls you into the higher octaves, where messages always offer balanced answers. Even the Devil has a soft spot in my heart as its information from the upper chambers asks us to be observers of our actions. The message is that our addictions and obsessions are creating disturbances that interfere with our life's plan. If the Devil shows up in a reading, it means the Divine Council is telling us we have grown comfortable with our obsessions and damaging compulsions. Its presence is asking us to choose different actions in the coming days. I'll have more of our Devil when we visit him where he lives in the lineup that follows. The following are souls who are in spirit who help me do good work in my readings. You have the same team, and after I introduce you to them, spend some quiet time getting to know them.

GUARDIANS

Guardians send out impulses of safety, signaling they are with us—to comfort us. I believe they are extras in the lineup of helpers on the other side. They are not assigned to us and don't devote a lifetime of service to one incarnated person. They are travelers who notice when a person is struggling, and stand close with hopes to give us confidence that we are safe and protected.

TEACHERS AND MENTORS

Teachers and Mentors give insights into what we can become, again, by giving us the impulse to certain beneficial and inspired actions. They encourage us to believe we are greater than we think we are now. They also reveal and encourage us to align with divine truth instead of our subjective truths. Their presence isn't static; they come and go, bringing inspiration and knowledge when we are focused on a certain task or goal. Call upon these beautiful beings when you find that creativity has slowed or stopped and when a project or relationship is at a standstill. They are souls that influence through epiphanies. One or two may take a liking to your goals and stay with you for quite a long time to help you achieve success.

GUIDES

Guides encourage us to act in congruence with the contract we agreed to before incarnating to achieve our full potential in this lifetime—sending impulses of encouragement for us to move in certain directions so life can synchronize beneficial opportunities. They help us choose wisely. Unlike Teachers and Guardians, Guides are not transient, but permanent. Your Guide Team doesn't show up all at once; you hire them, so to speak, as you grow and start making choices on your own. It's my understanding that a person is born with one Guide who comes in and helps you anchor into your body from the expansive being you were before birth. Many refer to this Guide as their Guardian Angel. It's true there aren't many choices a newborn makes, but the first Guide on your team helps acclimate you. They are also the keeper of what Andrea Hess of *The Empowered Soul* calls the golden web. This is the memory system your soul re-creates at the beginning of every lifetime to help you remember the previous life's lessons. When we have trouble as adults, I often find something wrong with how a person's golden web was woven when first created for the current lifetime. Simply put, a person can misremember lessons, causing a disruption in their lives, and once recognized and adjusted can live a more positive one. I believe your first Guide is in charge of helping you keep that golden web viable and healthy and, if changes are needed, helps align you to the present incarnation's reality.

A person gathers Guides as they start making decisions in childhood. If a child starts making up their own mind early, then she or he will start having Guides coming in very young. If there is little opportunity for a child to make their own choices, then they will have a smaller Guide team. Most people have four to six Guides that will remain by their side throughout their life. Unlike the popular belief,

I've found Guides to be quite to the point, with little emotion. They have the contract you agreed to prior to incarnating, and they intend to influence you in hopes of fulfilling the agreed-to contract. They feel responsible for your success and, I've discovered, are quite serious and direct in their communications. They are very wise, and each has their own personality, but for the most part they aren't cuddly. I find them all about the business of this lifetime. They make wonderful targets to tap information from because the messages usually come through in very direct ways. You will enjoy unmistakable answers by way of knowing (the eighth dimension), visuals (sixth dimension), and sounds (seventh dimension). Try positioning your understanding of Guides by cutting out the lovey-dovey stuff and being very direct when dealing with them. Be prepared for some blunt and direct answers! I just love working with Guides this way, and approaching them with this new understanding will bring you incredible results.

ANGELS

On this list of divine helpers, Angels are the only ones that are not souls and have never experienced an earthly lifetime. Angels are God's thoughts and will come and go quickly in and out of existence and connection. When you request protection from Archangel Michael, for example, you are actually asking for a *station of divine help be opened and filled*. Any Angel can respond because it is the *institution* of Archangel Michael that is represented—not one specific Angel. The job of Angels is to inspire us by leaning us toward good. Angels actually make it possible for a person to "do no harm" by creating an atmosphere of truth that is available for us to *choose* to respond to. They don't hold it against us or lose faith in us when we don't listen. They remain devoted but are saddened when we give in to our own needs and knowingly disregard the needs of others.

If you struggle with building a relationship with each of the Tarot cards, ask your Divine Council to help you with perspective, associations, and understanding through their eyes and hearts.

The Journey of The Fool

THE FOOL.

The Fool opens the journey as the true and full expression of a novice's heart. When the Fool comes into focus within the reading, it's a notice of a delightful blessing coming your way. I have never been able to read what that blessing will look like, and I asked my Divine Council for the reason for this. I was told that if I saw the blessing, I would share the blessing, which takes away the client's chance for a fresh approach to it. Anything a person can anticipate will come from what has already been experienced by them, and when those opinions are formed, then biases are anchored, spoiling the whole surprise. This would take away the option to be delighted by and enjoy it with a child's heart when it does come. The Fool points to something fresh and new, absent of hardship, so there is zero bitterness, zero fear, and zero apprehensions. The reversed Fool shows that you would like something new and fresh in your life but don't know how to get it. If in a love reading and the relationship is established but having trouble, the reversed Fool shows that the person wants a fresh start but doesn't know how to go about creating it. The reversed Fool does not mean that someone is being foolish, but restless, and could possibly make rash decisions to *make* life create something new. This would be seen as an impulse to completely break up with someone in hopes of bringing back that loving feeling (as the song goes) and then coming back with new energies. The reversed Fool is risky but isn't necessarily a fatal blow, just a messy, disruptive one. If, in a love partnership, the Fool is with a Page of any suit close, you can add that this person is emotionally immature with the situation, and their reactions and choices will be adolescent at best. Understandable if the couple is young, but if you are speaking to people in their 30s and older, the reversed Fool and Pages together indicate that the person these cards are for simply isn't learning the hard lessons needed to have successful relationships.

I approach love relationships with certain assumptions that are added to the frame of reference. One assumption is that poor behavior motivated by extreme and unreasonable jealousy or insecurity is understandable for people just starting out. If the reading is for people in their 20s, I give them room to act out, but still address that the drama isn't needed to show you care or ask for attention. If, however, you are reading anyone outside that age group, you are dealing with stubborn patterns of self-sabotage, and your reading should be truthful, of course, but kind. I present it like this reading for an older couple: "Here he has the reversed Fool with other cards (Pages) supporting the message that his communication style, when it comes to matters of the heart, is stunted. It's like he can't find mature ways to tell you how he's feeling. I see this kind of behavior in less experienced people in relationships. What this combination says is that he would like new ways of living inside the relationship, more diversity in living, less routine, and more travel. He just doesn't know how to say that, but now you know, so you can help him define his frustration. Then, together, make changes to allow love to deepen."

I always see the upright Fool as a breath of fresh air and tell my client to have a hopeful heart that life is syncing up a big blessing, something new, shiny, and fun.

The Magician

THE MAGICIAN.

The Magician plainly shows that your client has all they need to proceed with any task or project. They have all the education and resources for success. They may be lacking confidence, and that's why it's important you share the message with lots of encouragement. We often don't know we have all the ability we need until after the task or project is over. Then we look back at the success and see we did indeed have what it took. Having the Magician show may indicate that your client, because of insecurities, may skip embarking on something new, but that something new is important and arranged in their life plan to experience. Life has entrusted you, their spiritual advisor, to deliver the message of encouragement toward something new. That the Magician in them will be able to handle it like an expert. This is the ultimate manifestation card encouraging a person to tap into their spiritual gifts to bring in whatever they desire. Change doesn't live inside our wishes and hopes, which are only a piece of the magic. A person's actions activate and bring in the things you want, both emotional and tangible.

Magician reversed is the other side of the coin and indicates destructive behavior that can erode partnerships of all kinds. If I have this guy reversed, it means there is gaslighting and manipulation going on. I want to be clear here. If you're reading your client's person of interest and the reversed Magician appears, you need to deliver the above message to your client so they can better prepare for the ongoing control from their partner. You, as the advisor, bring enlightenment of the manipulation to light, and even if your client denies that their partner does that, suggest you both set it aside and she can look at it later. The message is on the table and asks to be delivered, and I guarantee she or he will start watching for the signs of the corrosive behavior that they may have been missed before. On the flip side, if you are doing a reading about your client's life and the reversed Magician shows up, it gives you more information about your client. If you don't remember anything else, please remember this. Spirit is telling you that your client may not be giving accurate information and may be setting you up to fail. I wouldn't recommend you bring the reversed Magician up; just understand that the person in front of you most likely is not being transparent.

If your client asks if love is in her or his future and the reversed Magician shows and it looks like they will indeed meet someone, tell your client that for some reason it looks as if they may sabotage the meeting for some reason. If they ask how they would be doing that, just tell the truth. You will appear inauthentic to this new person. Encourage them to relax and be themselves. It can also indicate that she or he is trying to control and manipulate the topic (love, money, career, family, job) you're reading about. If your client is complaining about a love relationship or trouble with family or job, this card reversed will tell you why they are having the problems. How you would approach the reading is by saying something like "Spirit is saying that you are trying to steer the situation toward a specific outcome, and the outcome you are trying to manifest is not the best one for you. What's that old saying? If you want to make God laugh, tell him your plans." Encourage your client to let go of the rope of control and let it unfold without trying to give influence to a specific end. The outcome will be more in alignment to them and will bring about a greater benefit and bounty to them.

The High Priestess

THE HIGH PRIESTESS.

This beautiful being is the guardian of your intuition—a beautiful gatekeeper I call upon to attend every reading I do. She can see every step of the future but will give you only enough information about the next few steps toward success. The message is to trust your gut, not your heart. She is pointing to the fact that extreme emotion isn't the state you want to be in when needing to make decisions. She is feminine power and manages your inner spiritual life. It's been my experience that when the High Priestess comes into a reading regarding love in general, it most often reveals that your client is looking for a deeper spiritual union than what they have had in the past. If they are in a new relationship, someone they haven't known for long, the presence of this beautiful Priestess means she or he is feeling a wonderful spiritual connection with this new person. It's easy to hand your entire heart over to this new affair, but that is a dangerous thing to do when you don't know someone well. The feeling of spiritual connectedness with someone is so seductive that you will need to advise your client to use caution, not because this new potential partner isn't the right one, but because their actions, while under the influence of this exciting thread of anticipation, will give off an impression of desperation. The High Priestess could be telling you, as the advisor, that they have been seduced into an imaginary happily-ever-after future. And while it could be true that this new acquaintance may very well be the one, their actions will be the result of living in the future in their minds, and inevitably their impulse to talk about where their newly formed relationship is going comes into the conversation way too soon.

There are a couple of cards I've discovered that influence the High Priestess and make this situation of imaginary futures worse. They are the **Devil (obsessive and compulsive)** and the **7 of Cups (lots of ideas, not all based in reality)**. I actually like seeing the High Priestess reversed in a love reading focused on a new acquaintance, because it shows the client is focused on the material world and not on the dreamy nebulous world of the heart.

This unique interpretation of our lady of inner knowing, the High Priestess, is acquired after many hours of reading people (mostly women) who are painfully in the deep, one-of-a-kind, *this is it* kind of love with people who are just casual friends or people they have gone out with only a couple of times.

When doing a general reading and the topic is not love, this card shows a time of deep reflection on spiritual matters. But if the question is love and this one shows up, be cautious and sensitive when you tell your clients to get their heads out of the clouds. The same with finance and money decisions: keep your feet on the ground and make choices with your head and not your heart.

The Empress

THE EMPRESS.

The Empress is Mother Nature, Mother Earth, in charge of the seasons and our body rhythms, including pregnancy. While the High Priestess creates spiritual power, our Empress is in charge of the material portion of our choices. You will most often see the Empress pictured sitting in nature, because that is her domain. Whether she appears in love or business, she is the ultimate feminine authority, since she feeds all outside information through the filters of caring, nurturing, and supporting others. The Empress brings in the best for all, not only the one you are reading for. She asks you to have good questions in the moment, framed well. "What's your fascination, and will you follow it?" "Are you nurtured enough to nurture others?" She reminds you that creativity will lift sadness and worry. If **Empress (bounty)** comes through in a business or career reading, you can be sure there are many options for your client. Even if they can't see it or feel it. Watch which cards are around her. If the **Chariot (focus on one thing)** or the **7 of Cups (scattered thinking)** shows with the Empress, it means you need to shine a spotlight on the job or position you want. Don't let anything get in your way. If there are any cards that show scarcity, perhaps the **5 of Cups (feeling of lack)**, the **Empress (bounty)** is asking you to focus on what you do have, and nature will move back around in your favor, with many options. It can also mean you are not casting your net wide enough to take advantage of her generosity. Encourage your client to apply for their dream position, even if they don't feel qualified, because the **Empress (bounty and options)** says you are ready. If your client's question is about pursuing a career in spiritual work, this card is asking you to explore Earth magic, shamanism, and crystal alchemy. At least study it for a while, because there is something in those classes that will benefit them. If our Empress comes through in a love reading, your client is striving for a traditional relationship that progresses into a family dynamic. A feeling of home. If there are Pages of any suit around the Empress, you are quite fertile, and if not in a position to start a family, literally, be careful. The reversed Empress gives you the feeling you have no bounty and options available. This isn't true, of course; you may very well feel a sense of insecurity, but the options are still syncing up for you. While you wait, nurture yourself and care deeply for your home and garden, and soon your sense of balance will return.

The Emperor

THE EMPEROR.

The Emperor is the patriarch of mature masculine leadership in regard to the material world. Whereas the Empress is the creator of nature, the Emperor is the creator of industry, the military, and social leadership. It's been my experience that if your client is having trouble with authority, the Emperor (upright or reversed) will reveal it, bring it up and out, so it can be healed. If that isn't the issue at hand and he comes through reversed, ask your client if they are having problems at work. Since this card represents the ultimate authority, if your client is in management and this card is reversed in the reading, tell them they are being perceived as an oppressor or bully. Reassure them that you understand they only want the best for their business and staff, but that intention isn't how their behavior is coming across to those around them. If the reading is for love or money, the Emperor tells you that a level-headed and practical path will serve you well. If reading for someone's person of interest, remembering that this is a snapshot of time, tell your client their person is all business and work and may be taking the front seat for a little while. If strong cards are around the Emperor, then it magnifies the already bold and dominant nature. See if the **Tower (collapse of the old)** comes after this card, since it can indicate that your client is pushing too hard, and the situation, love or money, will break and restructure. If the **Devil** is present, it points to the **obsession** with **dominance**, so if this is a love reading, this information is good to know. If this combination is answering a work question and reading is a subordinate, then talk about the underlying feelings of resentment toward authority and encourage them to consider starting their own business. The topic—be it love or money—doesn't really matter; the Emperor is the tradition of structures and established norms. This means that if upright, for love, this card says the person you are reading respects the tradition of society, and marriage is looked upon positively.

The Hierophant

THE HIEROPHANT.

To recap, the Empress speaks of the laws of nature, the Emperor is the keeper of traditional protocols regarding industry, and the Hierophant holds the leadership of formal religion. Hierophant speaks of orthodoxy and the teachings of sacred-text doctrine. Somewhat like the Emperor, when doing a love reading and the client wants to know more about someone they just met, the Hierophant upright means that the person of interest leans more toward traditional religious values held in society. In other words, a person who adheres to societal norms of timing in relationships will court a person for a certain amount of time, then become exclusive, then engaged, and then married. If perhaps the Hierophant hits the reading reversed, it has been my experience that either the person in question is not interested in a progressive relationship toward marriage or, quite simply, the dating relationship has not matured enough for the card to appear upright. That means the person of interest may very well enjoy the thought of marriage in the future, but the relationship is so new that affections haven't grown strong enough to entertain the thought of marriage. This information is so important in a new relationship because refraining from deep intimacy so sexual tension gets stronger will focus this new partner to shift from practice boyfriend/girlfriend to proper partner.

The Lovers

THE LOVERS.

The Lovers card shines the light on all collaboration that has a passionate component to it. Because of the title, most people see this as meaning only passionate sexual love, and indeed there is room for this interpretation; however, a broader perspective would serve you well, since this card truly symbolizes an enthusiastic collaboration between opposites and the clearing up of discrepancies. When reading a love question such as "I met this guy four weeks ago, and I want to know how he feels about our relationship," this one card (without the suit of Cups; emotions, around) may be a little disappointing since it points to him feeling sexual toward her but not emotionally connected. If I see the Lovers card, I can assume there is a healthy degree of sexual attraction for my client. However, if I don't see cards around the Lovers supporting emotional love (again, Cups, for the most part), then my interpretation is that his level of devotion is superfluous and purely physical at this time. It could very well be that his feelings of deep emotional love have not yet eclipsed the raw physical attraction, and there may be an uneven sentimental investment on his part regarding this intimate union. To be clear, when reading this particular card, and for many questions about love, you will need to look at supporting or contradicting cards to make sure you are intuiting the full picture for your client. For instance, if there is the **reversed Hierophant (not looking for marriage),** the **Devil (obsession),** and **no Cups (emotions)** present, you have someone who is interested in a friends-with-benefits connection. Once that kind of relationship is established, it will be hard to level up into a proper exclusive, progressive relationship. If there are any one of these Cups present, the **Ace of Cups (new love), 2 of Cups (relationship/collaboration),** or **9 of Cups (wishes come true),** as well as the **10 of Cups (emotional satisfaction),** you have met a viable partner interested in a healthy relationship. If the reading is about a career or job, the Lovers reveals a project or collaboration of great interest coming into view.

The Chariot

THE CHARIOT.

The Chariot can mean travel and transportation over land. It means fast-moving energy toward a goal, as long as both your horses are pointed in the same direction. As metaphor moves into literal, most decks depict this card with two different-colored animals, representing opposing forces that you, as the driver, need to somehow join into a common ambition or objective to create success. This card appearing in the reading tells you that you can achieve success through sheer willpower and control, which admittedly takes intense focus and discipline. This card shows that you can master opposing forces in a fractured team at work or a broken family situation and bring them together. Like many of us, our own struggle with challenges is what enslaves us, not the situation itself. When paired with **Judgment (karmic/reunions),** the **6 of Cups (people from long-ago past),** or the **10 of Pentacles (family legacy),** or a combination of these, you can be sure there will be a coming together of the family or old friends for one reason or another. The **Chariot (gathering control to move forward)** followed by the **reversed Ace of Pentacles** means that whatever tangible project you are on hasn't been thought through all the way yet. If this shows up during a relationship reading, it means you should probably wait until you are better prepared to move forward. The following combination has always been true for me. The **reversed Chariot (losing control over a situation)** and the **reversed 9 of Cups (overindulging in alcohol or other drugs)** will forewarn actions with consequences. You don't just shout out and declare that your client will drink and drive and then get into an accident, but mention to be prudent when celebrating and ask someone else to drive if you drink. If **Justice (legal system and contracts)** is present in the same throw, this could be a DUI kind of thing. The old saying "Try not to move so fast your Angels can't keep up" is a lighthearted and a cautionary message to deliver. Don't be a doom-and-gloom psychic or throw out dire predictions, because your advice can be all that's needed to shift this trajectory. I feel that enlightenment happens in an instant, so trust your clients to understand and choose their own future. Plus, you, as an advisor, have a huge responsibility to care for your client's emotional health while in your care. Even people who may not totally believe in what you do still have their hearts open to what you say. You can say a million wonderful things about them and their future and one negative, and I guarantee that one negative thing is what they will remember and talk about to others.

Strength

STRENGTH.

Strength gives you the energy to endure and overcome deficiency and frailties. This card is adorned with a beautiful woman who, through grace and patience, has tamed a lion. It acknowledges the difficulties and suffering you have endured to grow your inner strength and, to this end, excellence in moral courage. You have tamed the beast within, not by force but by gentleness. Whenever this beautiful card shows in a reading, it indicates that Spirit is asking you, as a reader, to tell the client their efforts have been noticed by the higher powers, and they have earned an unspoiled thread of grace to help them remain at peace. There are a few cards in the Major Arcana that take a pause from the sometimes rigorous journey from Fool to World. On your path from novice to excellence, the path has a few places to rest and recharge. This is one of those places (Temperance is the other card of rejuvenation and evaluation, but we will get to that one in a moment). Strength points to a person's natural ability to rise above conflict. In general, when a challenging situation happens, it's our human nature to participate in emotional stress and drama by trying to control it instead of trusting that lessons will unfold in right time.

The Strength card acknowledges that your client is looking at their problems from a healthy distance with a well-rounded perspective or is afforded the option to do so. The cards around Strength will tell you whether they have achieved it or should tap into it. If there are Pentacles close, you will know this thread of grace will help you cope with uncertainty regarding money, job, or relationships. It shares that unseen forces are working on your behalf behind the scenes and trust the support is there. **Strength (grace under pressure)** and the **4 of Pentacles (feeling insecure about not having enough)** come up often in my readings. I reassure my clients that they do indeed have enough to make ends meet, and that I understand there may not be a lot left over. Strength assures that blessings are on the way. To stay patient and concentrate on calming your emotions from anguish and unshakable strength will unfold a miracle. **Reversed Strength (not aligned)** shows that a person conflicted by what they feel on the inside isn't lining up with what they show others on the outside. This card reversed doesn't mean that anything needs to be corrected. Many times when we visit with others, or when at work, we don't allow our struggle and confusion with the things happening in our lives to show. We don't want our vulnerabilities to be on display in inappropriate places. It does mean, however, that your client needs to practice extreme self-care when not in performance in their daily lives. No matter what cards are around this card, Strength will shore you up and keep you going in the right direction.

The Hermit

The Hermit is a soul in solitude; however, this solitude is not an option but Spirit *insisting* you retreat into the silence of good council and spiritual contemplation. If you betray this request from the higher-ups and, instead, power through with the business of your day, you will feel like you're **faking it (Hermit reversed)**. You attend events or go to your job with a feeling of being an impostor, a plastic shell. To rise above the empty feeling of this particular life rhythm, it would serve you well to withdraw from activities and distractions of the world. This is critical to understanding who you are at soul level in relation to everything in your life. At times (looking at the other cards in the throw), the Hermit shows up in a reading and isn't asking the client to withdraw from all activity but rather offers a caution for her/him to hold back from pursuing a specific friend, concept, or project at this time. If reading a person of interest for a client in a love reading, and the question is "We had a fight, and I haven't heard from her/him for days—should I contact them?," the Hermit in the reading is saying absolutely no. To follow this person into their private spiritual solitude will never pay off. When Hermit appears in your client's reading, Spirit is asking them to look for their own council of teachers and guides. It's smart of you to turn off music and shutter outside noises as best as you can, to hear the soft whispers of advice and guidance. **Hermit (quiet contemplation)** paired with the **World (triumph)** is easy to read. Success and joy come out of contracting from life long enough to reassess who you are and what matters to you. If the upright **Hermit (contemplation)** and a bunch of party cards such as the **3 of Cups (social fun)** or the **9 of Cups (celebrations)** show, the Major cards in this lineup are expressing what the soul needs, and, if it's not reversed, you should enjoy yourself while out but arrange some silence and "free creative thinking" time when home to rejuvenate. If Hermit is reversed, then going out will feel like you're just going through the motions and putting in your time that you are obligated to do. Setting your world on mute will allow the soft messages from Spirit to be delivered and understood by you. Any cards of lack, **5 of Pentacles (a tendency to overspend)** or **reversed 6 of Pentacles (unable to give/share)**, will tell you what you will be correcting or shifting if you take a break from outside influence. If reading for someone who asked about the development of a new relationship and the upright Hermit shows, it means their person of interest will need alone time, maybe more than your client has the patience for. Usually, the **8 of Swords (feeling at no choice)** comes in saying that the POI may not be up for the expectations a proper relationship will need them to align with. Don't rush.

The Wheel of Fortune

WHEEL of FORTUNE.

The Wheel represents the cycles of life and signals that an uptick in good fortune is coming your way. It's the ultimate good-luck card and always a pleasant and welcome sight in a reading. You have put something in motion (you may or may not remember what it is) that will be paying off. This says destiny has orchestrated an unexpected and positive turn of events. If the supporting cards are negative, it doesn't necessarily mean good fortune isn't available—more like the client is doing something to sabotage the situation and dodging this beneficial destiny. Are you so comfortable with the familiar that you are turning away from something new? Or is it your low self-esteem making you feel like an unworthy benefactor of such good fortune? Upright or reversed, the Wheel will brighten up any part of the reading it sits around. Even if the **Devil (obsessive/compulsive)** or **Tower (breaking down the old to build new)** shows, you can count on the Wheel of Fortune to lighten the burden and the message. I can have an entire throw of challenging cards and lift the message to a much lighter level of hope and blessing if the Wheel comes in. In other words, whatever the hardship faced now will be short lived. Caution, controversy ahead. You will read in other Tarot books that the reversed Wheel means the opposite, that whatever was set in motion, be it conscious or unconscious, will turn out badly. After thousands of readings, I simply haven't found this to be true. I am not saying others are wrong. I am asking you to try each perspective and choose for yourself. I'm sharing how my Guides and I have understood this after years of practice reading it both ways. I'm sharing only those that have proven correct for me. If you, as an advisor, remain flexible with your declarations of truth and meaning, you too will develop your own language with your Guides.

Justice

Justice speaks to you about the legal matters in your life, from the simple handshake agreements to binding contracts and all matters of the court, be they civil or criminal. It asks you to look at all the facts and weigh them fairly against one another to reach balanced conclusions. This card suggests you are calm and deliberate when taking any action. It is a reminder to pause and allow enough time to ensure that fair-minded decisions are offered and executed. Divide equally all property, money, or settlements. If perhaps Justice is reversed, it has been my experience that the person you're reading for may feel they are on the unfair or unjust side of a decision or situation. They may feel angry or resentful, and the supporting cards in the reading will tell you the full story. If Justice is reversed, it commonly means a delay in the process. If paired with Pentacles, most often it represents documents, and the specific Pentacle card will tell you what kind. For instance, if the 10 of Pentacles stands with Justice, then most often it points to contracts and agreements with family or inheritance. If paired with the **Hierophant (traditional religion)** or **Empress (cycle of life)**, most often I read this as a marriage document or birth certificate. If the **Justice card (balance/contracts)** seems like an outlier, meaning you don't feel it fits the reading, then it's Spirit reassuring your client that they are being fair-minded with their assumptions and intuitive hits. Unlike the **Wheel of Fortune reversed (still an uptick in good fortune)**, or the **reversed Justice (broken promises and agreements)**. There have been times when, during a career reading, a client asks if they will be hired for their position of choice. If the answer is yes (laying down five cards with the yes/no spread), but I have the reversed Justice, I tell them that not everything discussed in the interview will end up in writing. If this lineup is with the **5 of Wands (gossip)**, I also add not to be quick to make friends at the new office with coworkers. We all want to be liked in a new place, but the reversed Justice coupled with, well, any 5 means they are being hired during a time of transition or conflict in the area they will start work in. Nothing awful, just a heads-up to withhold and not reveal too much of your private or career self. Many times this combination can be a message that management will be watching to see if you might be administrative material. Needing to be everyone's friend at a new job isn't going to give the impression of independence to upper management. I gave this very advice to a client who later told me that everything I mentioned came to pass. She did indeed get the job as predicted, and even though it felt really weird not to accept lunch invites from coworkers, she still resisted due to the caution given in her reading. The interesting part was what happened three weeks after she got hired. The very people who were so anxious to befriend my client got fired, and my client's position was reevaluated, with her job description shifting to her benefit. She said she normally shows overt delight to anyone who shows her interest in a new company, mainly because, like all of us, she wanted to be well liked, and she was normally a really upbeat person. But she resisted her norm, because the reading suggested that she would notice a few workers who would seem anxious to tell her gossip stories about the company and other staff members. She would act distracted or in a rush, and it all paid off. So, reversed Justice speaks volumes on any topic. What will it mean in love? That's an easy one. Even though our Lady Justice means contracts in a very tangible way, she can also show broken expectations and assumptions you wanted another to uphold. Relationships live in the tangible category, the Pentacle suit. Love relationships start and emote from the Cups, but agreements, especially unspoken ones, can bring in reversed Justice. There should be supporting cards such as the **10 of Swords (betrayal)**, the **3 of Cups (heartbreak)**, or even the **7 of Wands (defending one's position)**, but make no mistake: the cards around Justice will tell you everything. Often, I'm asked to read a client's boyfriend because he hasn't been texting as much, and she has fears he's losing interest. If, after I see the above circumstance and explain what is distracting him, she responses with "That can't be true; he hasn't said anything like that was happening in his life," kindly remind her that this reading was through her boyfriend's energy and not hers. This reading is for their person of interest and not them. This information of a complicated financial matter could very well hold the key to their reconciliation, since it explains that his distance has nothing to do with his affections for her.

The Hanging Man

THE HANGED MAN.

The Hanged Man is also known as the Hanging Man, picturing a person upside down who is feeling stuck and can't make a decision. This represents someone trying their best to see the problem from a different angle so they can have all the information before moving forward. This card is much like the Hermit because of its solitary nature; however, the difference is that the Hermit is life insisting a person stop and separate themselves from everything to gain spiritual knowledge, and the Hanged Man offers the choice to stop and separate from all to achieve a different perspective regarding situations, people, and projects. The Hanged Man means surrendering your desired control over outcomes, most often indicating the letting go of old patterns that aren't serving you now. In the past, these old patterns gave you a sense of security, but now, to stay true to yourself, you choose differently. If perhaps this card lands in reverse, it indicates that the person this reading is for will be resistant to make the necessary changes to move forward and make a decision. This leaves them and others hanging in the wind, waiting on them to choose a path. Of all the readings I have done on love, the **reversed Hanged Man (not willing to make the necessary changes to improve the situation)** most often represents a partner acting immaturely both socially and emotionally in regard to the situation at hand. If for money, it can show good old-fashioned stubbornness on the client's part. This makes you, the advisor, the person whom life has picked to point out new ways of thinking to ultimately encourage her/him to make choices that will better serve them, ultimately getting them closer to their goals. The most profound pattern I've noticed in readings about love is that the reversed Hanged Man may start out right after a fight and then right itself later if given enough time to pull ego and pride out of the way and look at the other person's perspective more clearly. How you would present this is "I see that because the fight or argument remains fresh in his mind, he's digging into whatever declarations were spoken during the squabble. If you see the **Wheel of Fortune (uptick in good fortune)**, the **Sun (everything is in the light)**, the **World (an indication they will rise above the adversity)**, and any **Ace for any suit (new beginnings)**, you can trust that the reversed Hanging Man you see today will right itself in the next few weeks. Quiet time is needed for this revelation. I mentioned earlier that I felt this card had a mature and immature nature. Those who are able to hear someone else's opinion that is different from their own will pause and consider the other's position, then renegotiate the problem. This will be evidenced as the upright Hanged Man and the more mature, positive card. The immature is the **reversed Hanged Man (resisting change, not even hearing of change)**, revealing a hurt pride or the inability to articulate and negotiate cognitively in a discussion. They shut down and won't participate, speak, or address the topic without retreating for days or weeks, without a guarantee that the time alone will bring about a change of heart. Look to the rest of the throw for that answer. Any card that shows positive forward movement can comfort the client that their person of interest looks as if the quiet time he needs to take will be to the benefit of the relationship. The cards that indicate that there won't be a change of heart follow. This list is not complete, but you will get the idea. **Reversed 8 of Wands (no forward movement)**, **reversed Page of Swords (delay in progress)**, or the **Devil (obsessive compulsive)** means that this person may not be able to get to the other side of the problem because he is unable to forgive any perceived wrongdoing against him.

On a separate note, I've mentioned earlier the **reversed King and Queen of Swords (mean-spiritedness)**. If the Hanging Man is close to either of these, it means that one or the other went too far in the argument, that there was a pause but they couldn't just let the room breathe. They had to have the last word, possibly not feeling that their struggle had been adequately recognized and acknowledged by their partner. Then you have a whole other reason for the reversed Hanging Man, prompting a new conversation with the client.

Death

The Death card means the natural ending of a cycle—not literally the ending of life. This card tells you to release the past, take time to mourn it, and then move forward to a fresh new beginning. This is a time when change can't be avoided. When it is upon you and you're going through the letting-go process, this card promises that something better is coming soon. It's my belief that Spirit never allows bad to happen where good can't come from it. Look at all aspects of life, love, job, and career, as well as friends and family, through the filter of who or which situations make your edges (emotions) feel tired and worn out. Look also at how you behave or interact in these situations. It's time to let go of what you think you know, and to embrace a new way of living. *Your old ways and treatment of others may need to pass away for the blessing of a lighter version of you to finally be revealed and serve the world as intended in your soul's blueprint.* In a love reading, **Death (natural ending)** means that the person in question, simply put, feels this is an exit point and doesn't have a need to assign blame. Death card is finite in relation to how you love another or how you feel and act inside a project, job, relationship, etc. We all go through phases of this card when growing a relationship. It doesn't necessarily mean the couple will break up, but it screams the heavenly need for things to change drastically. Interestingly, I have discovered that the **reversed Death card (not giving up what should go)** isn't a bad card but indicates that the person we are reading knows that the relationship (or project, or investment) isn't going well and should come to an end, but feels there is something left to catch fire again. Here's the rub. The reversed Death means that person feels there is more to the relationship, insisting that things remain the same in expectation and obligation. They want everything to stay the same and for things to just get better on their own. This reveals a person who doesn't know how to reinvent him- or herself to create a fresh start, while the reversed Death card *requires* a completely new start. You will not be successful in resurrecting whatever situation the Death card is addressing without considerable changes. I've been asked to address what it means if **Death (natural ending)** is paired with **Judgment (reaping what you sow / resurrection)**. It has been my experience that Judgment doesn't carry the weight to resurrect and make possible a successful relationship without huge changes happening within it. Judgment may indicate a sincere desire to call again, to fix, to negotiate by one or the other to try again. It can indicate someone contacting the other for so-called closure but doesn't guarantee a happily ever after if both aren't willing to make big shifts. What is that magic shift? The couple needs to identify themselves inside the institution of the relationship and not the solidarity of the individual. As I said, big changes will be needed for success. An interesting observation is the difference between **Death (natural ending)** and the **8 of Cups (walking away from something you've put a lot of time and energy into)**. Both speak of a relationship or project ending, but the difference is that with **Death**, a person feels a **sense of completion**, a feeling that a season has come to a close. A little sad maybe, but walking away and quitting feels calm and right. The **8 of Cups** says that a person has struggled with a situation that has taken them so far away from who they thought they were that they *had* to **leave** or forever lose the sense of who they are. With the 8, a turning and walking away creates a spark of joy and excitement for the future as a strong and independent person. This is a subtle difference, yes, but this nuance will help you accurately explain the state of mind their person of interest has so your client can make good choices for their own health and well-being.

Temperance

Temperance (moderation and patience) advises you to quietly steer your horse (pride and ego) toward the middle lane for the day. Be measured in your actions and keep your nose out of everybody else's business. Don't push your opinion on anyone and don't move close to the edges for debate on any topic; in other words, temper your impulses to control. She represents the constant interaction of the spiritual and material worlds, an ongoing process to raise the dense earth while mixing the blessings of heaven, creating the promised equilibrium between good and evil so that we—inside our human experience—can enjoy the luxury of choice. When Temperance appears, she is advising you to watch and learn from others without conditions or favor, since there is something valuable for you in whatever is going on right now. At this moment in time, you are the student, not the teacher. Can't think of many other cards in the deck that advise so clearly on what your next steps should be. The reversed Temperance doesn't mean you are not patient; it does, however, caution that the situation ahead may be bumpy and not to fight against it. It's been my experience that the reversed Temperance and the upright are about the same, both advising you to have patience and not push the river. The reversed Temperance speaks about the situation ahead and that it may require attention and effort to stay calm and steady. I love Temperance since it is one card in the deck that I feel offers an option to choose peace and longevity regarding whatever topic you are researching. She is constantly pouring silver into gold and back again, always in motion and never out of balance. The other longevity card is Judgment, since it speaks to us on a karmic level and may even go into past lives, if an advisor feels the ability to read from that perspective.

THE DEVIL.

This is not an indication that all the devils from the gates of hell are on their way to you. No, it doesn't mean that evil is coming from the outside of you. It means that your own personal devils *you* have hired to accompany you that manifest through *your* actions are close, and the Devil's presence forewarns you are about to sabotage the situation at hand. This is a card that affects all other cards around it in a negative way, pouring a dark shadow on everything because it signals that addiction of all kinds is active or will become activated soon. It's about feeling enslaved and fixated by your choice of drugs, alcohol, overeating, shopping, or depending on anger and violence (and that's just the short list) to dominate how you get your way with others. The Devil shows you when you may be obsessing over another person, project, or material thing. This card shows, in no uncertain terms, that your client or the person of interest you are reading is on a destructive path that will slow down all momentum for success and happiness. It is part of the social and ethical equilibrium that Temperance speaks of, and when you see this in a throw, it says to pay attention to your thoughts because not all of them will be your own. Be on notice that something (jealousy, envy, resentment, spite, or greed, to name a few) may be carrying you away, and it's time to self-reflect and course-correct. As with any addiction that can overwhelm and hijack the emotional integrity of a family, workplace, and personal life, it is clear you may not be in as much control as you thought. If I'm doing a love reading and the client is asking about a loved one, I tread lightly because the client sometimes won't recognize the problem if they have been living with it for a while. We can become desensitized to the problem. If the **reversed 9 of Cups (excess)** has the **Devil (compulsive obsession)** in the throw, then the person we are reading most likely is using substances to cope with the current situation, and those coping mechanisms will sabotage and slow the healing. If the client says her person of interest is sober, this combination *does not* mean this person has broken their sobriety and commitment to recovery. It does mean that the same impulses that drove them to their destructive behavior are present, and they may be struggling but not necessarily failing.

The reason the Devil card darkens every other card in the reading is that a person's obsession is with them in every situation. If there are a lot of Pentacles in the reading, for example, you can be confident that their judgment on what to do with money, investments, or even home improvement tasks will be negatively affected. Another Devil can be recognized as the obsessive nature of an artist who has been categorized as a genius but exhibits the risk of self-harm. In general, if the Devil card is ill dignified, or if you have cards that you would read as negative or challenging, the Devil will make it worse. Some unfortunate combinations are the **Moon (illusion)** or, worse, the **reverse Moon (deceit of others / self-deception)** or **10 of Swords (victimhood)**, and **any 5 of any suit**. The messages will be louder and point the way for this person to lose control. **Devil and 5 of Cups (regret with possible self-harm)**, **5 of Swords (conflict/destruction)**, **5 of Wands (competition)**, and the **5 of Pentacles (poverty mentality)** all are made more extreme when the Devil is close. If you have positive cards, such as the **Sun (pleasure, vitality)** or the **World (success)**, **Judgment (reunion, healing)**, or **10 of Cups (emotional happiness)**, the Devil will make them less effective, since the addiction makes those blessings seem unattainable even though they are arranged in their favor right in front of them.

Tower

THE TOWER.

The Tower is one of the most unwelcome cards since it represents unwelcome change. Most books describe it as catastrophic ruin, since it points to sudden and swift changes that go against our human nature of striving to live within a sense of security at all costs. As ominous as this sounds, I have discovered that most readings containing the Tower show that my client has an intense desire to control a situation that isn't supposed to be manifested, and a change in perspective now, at the time of the reading, can offset harsher life lessons down the way. The Tower can indeed signal a sudden job loss or accident that causes financial stress and will set on fire any and all worn-out structures that aren't serving you any longer. This card demands that you pay attention and free yourself from assumptions and expectations you have of yourself and others. You need to step back far enough to see if that job (the one you just got fired from) truly reflected your life's joy-filled fascinations. Most often, I have found that long before you find yourself inside the turmoil of a Tower, life has whispered messages to course-correct, messages to reevaluate what you think you need in life to be happy. A visual I like to share regarding the Tower is one of God picking you up by the back of your collar and lifting you out of a comfortable situation (comfortable but not aligned with your soul's contract) and gently swinging you back and forth. Even though the movement feels unwanted at the time, you notice that all the misaligned thoughts and theories that were insisting on strict rules of preservation start to fall away. As this situation calms, you start trusting that life is placing you where you are supposed to be, remembering that Spirit never allows bad to happen that good won't come of it. Once your Tower has fallen, you can rebuild using only the bricks that will truly serve you this time. Choosing only the bricks that reflect your moral and ethical truths will reestablish a sense of security and even boost your self-esteem and worth. You can, with the information you receive in the reading (reflected in the surrounding cards), voluntarily dismantle your Tower (being open to new perspectives) and throw away the bricks that are threatening to fall anyway. One way or another, the bad bricks (false beliefs) holding your Tower up will break away, either by your own choices or through the power you have bestowed your teachers, guardians, and guides from the beginning. Your agreement to live within your soul's blueprint matters most. You came to Earth for a reason, and the occasional Tower events ensure you stay within the agreement set up for this lifetime.

Tower energy is *subjective* and not always in the reading to tell your client that something out of the blue is coming and threatening their feelings of security. That's a horrible message in any form. The rest of the cards for that reading will give you plenty of information showing a path to peace. Here are some examples. **Tower (unwanted change)** with the **5 of Pentacles (poverty / sense of lack)** is a perfect example. While I was teaching a class, one of the students got this combination and gasped, having just learned the traditional meaning and calamitous power of the Tower. The rest of the students fixated on this combination and collectively summed up that chaos was definitely in her future. I reminded everyone that the 5 of Pentacles was only a 5, and that the sense of not having enough money to weather whatever the Tower has set up for her was just in her mind. The 5 of Pentacles is a reminder that we have more resources than we think. I then asked everyone to look at some of the other cards in the spread: The **Chariot (focused project/travel)**, which is most likely her car, and the **7 of Pentacles reversed (financial problem will not take from savings)**. That was backed up by the **6 of Pentacles upright (plenty on hand)**, showing that she will have enough to be able to pay out of pocket. To sum it up, I told her she would have something out of the blue on a financial level, but not to get overly concerned about it, since it is a minor inconvenience. Later that summer I went over to this student's house for a visit, and she brought this reading up, saying she was flabbergasted about how accurate it was. As this particular reading, with the Tower and Chariot worked out, she told me her car didn't start one day. She had it towed to the shop, where the mechanic discovered that the entire electrical system had been destroyed by mice (she lived in the county on acreage with lots of critters). She nearly fainted when he told her it would be a $5,000 job and she would have to leave it for several days. He walked away but turned back, saying, "Oh, and I forgot to tell you that your insurance will pay for it. I see this a lot in the area, and there is never an issue with payment." She had to pay only a small deductible, not having to touch her savings, just like the reading promised. The thing to remember is that the **Tower (sudden and unwanted change)** doesn't always mean crippling circumstances are coming your way.

The traditional meaning of the Tower card is a sudden, unwanted change, but I would like you to lift the burden of such a prediction off that particular meaning and interpret it like this—especially if the Tower is contrasted by positive and light-hearted cards. I think of the Tower as a moment coming up when a person feels they don't have a choice or options. Something out of the blue that pulls your attention quickly. We have little Towers happening all the time, especially if you have kids! A child's Tower can be the hot-glue gun breaking before the art project is done. A sudden surprise that is very disappointing, because the child doesn't have the freedom or resources to fix the problem on their own. They need to raise the alarm to a parent and negotiate a prompt solution right in the middle of their creative expression! How disappointing is that? To us, all the grown-ups in the room, this seems like a silly thing our kid has gotten all worked up about, but that's because adults have choices, options, and resources. Our little creative genius doesn't.

The reversed Tower is something different altogether. I read this the same way I read the reversed Hanging Man, which is a person who is not willing to make the necessary changes to improve a situation. We all have known people who seem to live in a panic, saying they never have options and that every life shift, large or small, creates overwhelming challenges. The reversed Tower tells you, the advisor, that the problem brought to you today may be an old pattern grown and nurtured either by your client's stubbornness toward change or a level of comfort with chaos. But good news! You now know the secret of the reversed Tower and have an opportunity to change your client's perspective about the situation at hand. It does take a nuanced delivery, to be sure, since there must be a lot of sensitivity approaching the problem in such a different direction. I would say it like this: "The presence of the Tower reversed shows me there is a pattern developing with this situation. Maybe you are feeling you can never catch a break with money or love, and the problem feels like it keeps coming back." My clients always agree but rarely bring that up themselves. They will say it feels like *Groundhog Day*, starting something that then never seems to catch fire. The reversed Tower means that a *change of perspective* along with a *new action* is needed to make your love life or business career blossom.

The upright Tower with Pentacles means there may be a restructuring regarding money and possessions. If perhaps you see the **7 of Swords (deceit)** or **10 of Pentacles (feeling like a victim)** close to the **Tower (sudden change)**, then check personal and family finances. A Tower with love cards or Cups (relationship/friendship) means a restructuring, and new understanding is needed regarding the relationship. This can mean a proper relationship or a casual friendship. Interestingly, I've discovered that if a Tower is close to Wands, the recovery from this startling shift is really quick. The suit of Swords **(thought)** has a terrible time when faced with Tower energy. Swords tend to overthink everything anyway, but unfortunately, little forward motion comes into play with them. Just talk to your client about changing perspectives and encourage being the observer of their lives so they may lessen the impact the Tower brings.

The Star

THE STAR.

After the progression from addiction (Devil) to collapse (Tower), the Star comes in and gives hope after all the storms and promises better days ahead. Your creativity comes back, along with new spiritual understanding, shifting life so the magic of synchronicities returns. The warm wind of hope is at your back, moving you gently forward. This card symbolizes an end to problems, the proverbial light at the end of the tunnel. You remember that your life's purpose manifests through the divine gifts you bring to the world, and now they begin to reveal themselves. The lessons learned from past trauma serve you well, and life will ensure that you will have the opportunity to offer this wisdom to others. Every word is profound when the light of the Star is upon you. As poetic as our Star card is, you will find she is not grounded at all. The following will explain.

There are major cards that are close to Earth, such as the **Empress (Mother Nature / Earth magic), Emperor (business/corporations and hierarchy), Hierophant (structured religions), Hermit (personal solitude), Justice (contracts/agreements with others), Lovers (physical love), Chariot (travel by car / dominating your circumstances), Death (natural endings), Tower (sudden changes), Devil (obsessions), and World (triumph / completing tasks / celebration).** And then there are a group of major cards closer to heaven that have softer messages and less directional guidance and speak to a healthy state of mind and heart. Those cards are the **Star (hope)**, **High Priestess (being divinely faced)**, **Fool (a new childlike feeling)**, **Strength (the gift of grace under pressure)**, **Magician (manifesting)**, **Wheel of Fortune (blessings/synchronicities)**, **Hanging Man (pausing and thinking differently)**, **Temperance (staying neutral)**, **Moon (mystery/secrets)**, **Sun (success/ happiness)**, and **Judgment (karma / reaping what you have sown)**.

The Star card (hope) also indicates messages from Spirit. I have found that if the Star is with the **7 of Cups (fantastical thinking)** or the **4 of Cups (indifference)**, or both, your client may be participating in spiritual escapism, where their thoughts and choices aren't grounded enough to make low-risk decisions. If other cards in the throw are more grounded, the Star upright can mean that you recognize and understand that you are responsible for your own results, as well as having a good idea of your purpose in life. The reversed Star reveals your desire to integrate your divine self-expression into everyday life, and what you choose to do with your life (life's work) must reflect that divinity.

The Moon

THE MOON.

The Moon is all about emotions and, with that, illusions. When this mysterious card appears, it's asking you to be mindful of your imagination, since you are now susceptible and vulnerable to fear-based thinking. You become more aware of your emotions, and your keen psychic abilities will reveal more options for your life. But be careful with those options and make sure that you are centered and clear before settling on your personal declarations of truth. Moon is saying to sleep and center before deciding, since your emotions may be skewing the real picture, and your choice may not be viable in the light of day. This isn't a bad thing, because, for writers and artists, this is a time of increased imagination, so exploit it now for great success. Having the Moon card in your reading asks you to be quiet and watch people and dreams, understanding that life-altering decisions should be set aside for now since you just can't see the whole picture yet. Use this time instead to study the thread of light connecting you to others and to heavenly resources. In a love reading, the **Moon (illusions)** makes for a mysterious lover, partner, or friend. You feel as if you just aren't getting the whole story. The same for business, management, and coworkers. It isn't so much that you feel like the oddball, but that others are not filling you in on all the information you need. A reversed Moon can reveal gaslighting from your friend, coworker, or partner. This shows conscious mean-spiritedness and self-deception. No matter how much information you may think you are given during a reading, if the reversed Moon is present, it means that the person you are reading has not fully opened up, and their true intentions won't come into view. It won't matter how much you think you know about this person; there is more they aren't disclosing. Possibly some of the other cards may point to what the person is withholding, but you really can't be sure. If a person you are reading isn't interested in sharing themselves, then you won't be able to tap in completely. That being said, I've met very few people I haven't been able to read. There may be a bubble of protection over deep pain, though. When this happens, it would look like Moon upright or reverse, and all the other cards around it will be playful and lighthearted. Your person of interest is saying that everything is fine on the outside, and is private on how they feel about the situation on the inside. Here is a caveat: I have just rambled on about how suspicious you should be with the reversed Moon, but here is when it isn't that bad. If your client asks about someone *they've just met* and the Moon appears upright or reversed, it is completely natural, since a person doesn't tell a stranger all about themselves. My advice to the client when the cards unfold this way is not to hand their heart over too quickly, since there is something major they aren't revealing, and then I educate the client about the mysteries of this card.

The Sun

The Sun comes next and fills those shadowy illusions the Moon was casting with light that reveals the truth of all things. This one will brighten up all other cards in the reading, lightening up the negative ones and giving kind regards to all others. The Sun splashes happiness, clarity, and a large dose of impulse for carefree self-expression. You have just breathed in the creative and mysterious blessings of the Moon that the Sun will help you express in the written word, a dance, a canvas, a song, or a sweet cake. The world is anxious to see what you come up with, and you can trust that your work will be received well. This is a great time to start new projects and get across the finish line. This is a time to prosper, so look toward the horizon and follow the light of the Sun. The **Sun (bright future)** is always positive, but when it comes in reversed, it says the client *might not be feeling the positive energy*. This could be telling you they are blocking the light because of the habit of a negative thought pattern, but it certainly doesn't mean the light isn't available to them. The Sun is shining even reversed, so take your client by the hand (metaphorically) and walk them outside and into the healing rays. They will go willingly once you start describing the bounty of options coming their way.

Judgment

JUDGEMENT.

This is known as the karma card, one of rejuvenation and healing. It has been my experience when reading about lost love that if the **Judgment card (resurrection/healing/rejuvenation)** shares time in your reading, the answer will be one of reunion and redemption. Judgment says you reap what you've sown; all good actions spent inside your relationships, work, and projects have accrued, and the outcome will be in your favor. It is a time of healing and an awakening of self-realization and rebirth. With that, make the necessary adjustment to express who you truly are. The name of this card may give the impression that you are being judged, but it actually points more toward *benefiting from your past work*. No one outside of yourself is judging you harsher than you are. The Judgment card helps you back up far enough from any situation to see the perfection in it. Judgment asks you to look at your choices and life situation to determine what you will keep and what you don't want to live with anymore. What I've discovered with the many love readings is that Judgment really does mean someone from the past will be influencing the future of this client. If the question is "We broke up; is he or she coming back?," then if Judgment is upright, the answer will be yes; however, you need to read the rest of the cards in the throw to see if he or she will return with a changed heart or go back to the same troubles that broke everything up in the first place. Even though Judgment is healing and promises reunions, I need to see other cards that show it's worth the effort. If the other cards around Judgment say that they won't come back with a changed heart, and you still want to go out with them to make sure, by all means, go and have a good time. But keep your head over your heart and really notice what they say about the breakup. I never tell people whom to stay for, wait for, or leave. I tell my clients what they can expect in the next few months if circumstances remain the same. Then they can decide. If Judgment comes in reversed, then no matter how much the other cards say that they want to come back or they are grieving the loss of this love, they most likely will not reach out again. The person walking away and letting go of the relationship or project may be in terrible grief; they still have the momentum and determination to heal without going back. Here are the examples I run into if it looks like *they will be leaning back* into the relationship with a changed heart. Upright **Judgment (resurrection)**, along with a few of the following cards in the spread: **any Ace (new beginnings)**, the **4 of Wands (have built a strong foundation and don't want to give that up)**, **Wheel of Fortune (understanding that everything has ups and downs)**, **2 of Cups (passionate collaboration)**, **Knight or Page of Cups (a new way of expressing love)**, **Magician (manifesting abilities)**, **5 of Cups (guilt and remorse)**, **Hierophant (respect for the institution of partnership)**, **6 of Cups (sense of family)**, **Lovers (sexual desire)**, and **7 of Pentacles (what has already been tangibly accrued)**. The last one means that the couple may have joined resources, such as purchasing a house or car, or joined on a rental lease. What both of them have built together, and the partner doesn't want to walk away from that combined effort. A spread that *shows a partner not returning* is the **reverse Judgment (resistant to admit wrongdoing or a feeling that a partner is too critical)**, **4 of Cups (not interested or focused on success)**, **5 of Swords (critical words / arguing)**, **10 of Swords (feeling betrayed)**, **5 of Wands (bickering)**, **7 of Wands (defending their position)**, **2 of Swords (stalemate, not moving forward)**, **8 of Swords (feeling they have no choice in the matter)**, **8 of Cups (feeling relief it's over)**, and **10 of Wands (feeling like the burden to make the other happy is uneven)**. They feel they have done more than their share to make the relationship work: **5 of Pentacles (feeling of lack and hopelessness)** and **Hermit (going quietly within to discover the spiritual reasons of the hardship)**. I've discovered that Hermit energy doesn't call the next day. And **Death (your partner feels this is a natural ending)**.

You will have the same outcomes when reading for a job that has ended, or a decision to leave a career, and you want to know if they will have a change of heart. Another combination that has been accurate in predicting family reunions or visits with old friends is **Judgment (resurrection)**, the **8 of Wands (fast-moving energy, sometimes meaning air travel)**, **Chariot (sometimes meaning ground travel, by car, train, or bus)**, **6 of Cups (family of origin and old friends from long-ago past)**, and **10 of Pentacles (family legacy is paramount)**. The only caveat with this is the Chariot, since that card tells you that gathering enough resources to go to a family reunion or have a trip may be complicated. Remember that to have success with the Chariot, you need to get both of your horses focused and moving in the same direction to keep your Chariot moving. Both horses seem to be pulling in opposite directions. But when you do get your horses focused and your ducks in a row (couldn't help the animal metaphors), you will have great success. I had one reading where Judgment and lots of family cards such as the prior plus the Chariot were present. I mentioned that a family reunion or some kind of party celebrating with old friends is in the works. My client had many reasons why she couldn't entertain the thought of such an event. The first reason was that she didn't know of anything being planned, but she was sure she wouldn't be able to take time off work and go. Second was that her friends and family lived in different states and that she would be gone too long—she was concerned about her dog. The third was that time and money for that kind of excursion felt overwhelming. I suggested she think about it and not to count it out, since the cards are pointing to attending, and that it is acknowledged there are some things you need to plan for, but it's certainly doable. And, I added, "You will have a blast, so think about it." The next time I saw her, she told me that indeed a reunion was offered about a week after the reading, and because she had already been thinking about it, she not only said yes right away but decided to fly instead of drive so she would have more time to visit. The Chariot's message was that she could pull things together, even though it may feel too hard in the moment. Once the idea starting percolating, new options presented themselves, and the service from friends to help with house and pets opened up. It was so easy, she couldn't say no to going. There was a similar story I shared when I wrote about the suit of Cups—specifically the **6 of Cups (people from your past)** and the **10 of Pentacles (family legacy)**. This prediction is always fun, but even more so when the client isn't aware of anything being planned at the time of the reading.

The World

THE WORLD.

The World completes the road from the young novice with the heroic Fool's heart to a well-rounded and wise conclusion described by the World. Completing the circle to enlightenment, our hero has picked up many lessons through all the choice points along his journey. If this life's journey was expressed in a straight line, it would look like this:

0. **The Fool (you)**, starting projects and relationships with a childlike optimism

1. **Magician**, figuring out that you have all that is needed to manifest and create inside that project or relationship. Then on to

2. **The High Priestess**, who whispers secrets of heaven while you manifest.

3. **The Empress** teaches you, our lead star, about nature, how to grow a garden, care for animals, and create new life. Then step into corporate life with

4. **The Emperor**. It is at this point of your journey that you get your first taste of the real world and all its rules and regulations. You have grown enough to hold down a real, paying job that tests your tenacity of being a well-prepared subordinate and your ability to respect hierarchy. Emperor will create the opportunity to evaluate (your first real choice point) whether you are comfortable and thriving in structure or enjoy the freedoms of the artist's spirit. This card is the first one in the line of 22 majors where *you (the hero, and Fool)* test your critical thinking so as to choose what part of these two options you enjoy best—usually measured by how happy or unhappy you feel with the structure of the organized and controlled world. Staying true to yourself at this juncture will make the road ahead much easier. Which path did you take when thinking about what you wanted to do with your life? Did you choose the path of the entrepreneur / sole proprietor, or the graduating ladder of business where someone else measures your successes? Next, our Fool learns all the demands and requirements of structured religion evidenced by our

5. **Hierophant**. The Hierophant is the leader and metaphoric enforcer of earthly religious teachings. The young mind of our Fool is educated on how to relate to the world through man's interpretations of heavenly right and wrong. Next on the path to enlightenment comes

6. **The Lovers**, where you discover what it's like to be physically close to another person or completely passionate about a project or event. Here is where you are exposed to the intricacies of intimacy and, with that, all new emotions and expectations, both spoken and unspoken. The tricky part is remaining true to yourself in thoughts, morals, and ethics, stepping back from the black-and-white world the Hierophant teaches and, with this new exposure, to deep passion. This helps you better understand not only life, love, and work, but an awareness of others and their challenges. Here is when you step back from yourself and think of others on a regular basis building an important part of your character. Next on our path is

7. **The Chariot**. After looking outside yourself and focusing on the well-being of others, possibly for the first time in your life taught by the Lovers, life is demanding that you snap back and focus on where you are going with this new and valuable information. Chariot gives you lots of choices on how to get from point A to B, but you now need to control your situation to ensure that you get to your destination. Here is where you learn discipline and tenacity for the first time. The Chariot is your first taste of freedom, your first car, with all the expense and knowledge needed to pay for it and care for it. The cards are coming closer to Earth. In the beginning, we were lighthearted kids without a care in the world, and now we need to choose a job and a lover and start investing in tangible goods, such as a car, by concentrating on manifesting resources. This also metaphorically speaks to all investments: buying a home, for instance, with all the details and sticky threads it entails, such as disclosing so much of your life to get a loan, choosing a place, bidding on it, and packing your stuff. It's like herding horses that want to go in opposite directions. The inflexible contracts of ownership (and having structure and security as the reward) or the freedom you will feel just staying young and roaming around the planet with ease (giving up material security). When you were old enough for your first car, what were the challenges you faced as a young adult making your own decisions? Remembering this experience means you understand the Fool in the deck much better and where he is on his journey to enlightenment. As the numbers get higher, the stronger the messages and more mature our hero, you,

become. Once invested inside the world of manifested goods, a bit of panic sets in as you wonder if you can keep up with everything. You now know that paying for the car and the loan on the house requires trust that our job or way to make a living isn't disrupted. This is where

8. **Strength** comes in with a blessing of grace. This coming-of-age involvement in the world may seem to be quite uncomfortable for you. This is when the true meaning of faith comes in for the first time. A thread of power tethered to your first chakra (a sense of belonging to tribe and society) and second chakra (manifesting at the physical level) to move through any hardship with poise and dignity. All the changing circumstances with choosing a career, exploring physical closeness, and signing contracts, with the harsh reality that your possessions are yours as long as your job stays viable, can have you start questioning if the effort is worth it.

9. **The Hermit** is asking you to question if everything you are investing in is in alignment with who you are at soul level. This prompts Fool, you, to go within and be separate from people, then asking these hard questions: Am I a good and truthful person? Am I acting with authenticity by showing on the outside what I feel on the inside often enough to trust my ideals? Am I in charge of my own thoughts and actions, or am I influenced by others so much that I change my behavior to ensure they're comfortable around me? Another choice point. This is when real course correction takes place if you realize you're not fully embracing and, most of all, expressing to others your ethics, morals, and personal truth. If you choose at this point to keep your personal truth expressed only on the weekends and present yourself differently inside how you feel society expects, then the rest of your journey could be difficult. Some of this is fine and expected, but too much can make you uncertain of who you really are. Hermit gives you time to evaluate how anchored and balanced you are in the chaotic world. As you can see, each choice point on this road gets a bit tougher. When all seems so serious the

10. **Wheel of Fortune** rolls in to lighten the heart, since the last few cards have seemed quite serious. Wheel teaches that nothing stays dark forever, and not to approach the good times with a cynical attitude. We sometimes, at this point in life, train ourselves not to get our hopes up or never fully embrace happy times, because the next shoe will drop and spoil everything anyway. It's here that we learn that life is intended to be a soft flow like a river, mostly smooth

with a few rough patches. Those rough patches caused by rocks (challenges and restrictions) are designed to slow you down enough to consider all options. They aren't designed to stop us completely, even though it feels that way at times. Farther down the lane toward enlightenment we see

11. **Justice** redirecting our focus to the contract you agreed to before incarnating, and to remind you that problems really do level out eventually. Lady Justice grants you permission to stop and filter your opinions of all circumstances through a symmetrical lens. Justice insists you be fair in your assessments and views of life in all its expressions.

12. **Hanged Man** (or Hanging Man) asks you to pause all forward momentum and think about how you can do things differently. To turn down the volume of chaos and consider how others may feel about you or the situation at hand. To see how and where others fit in your life and their own. This is the time to consider the needs, wants, and desires of others besides yourself. By mirroring back another person's best self for a change, shining the light on them and not yourself. Selflessness is what is being taught, and if Fool does what is asked, a sound maturity sparks and grows into a positive force for everyone standing close. The point in time we all can relate to in alignment with the Hanged Man is the point of discovery, understanding that we are responsible for our own results. I was about 20 when Justice visited and I learned this, and boy, it was a tough lesson. I had been let go from a job, and I needed to complain about the unfairness to a friend. I was in the middle of explaining how awful I was treated by everyone, which in turn made me not do my job very well. *They* were the ones who made me lose my job. My friend let me have it with both barrels, and to this day she doesn't remember talking to me about it at all. She told me in no uncertain way that I was the only one who did anything to cause the loss of my job. "It doesn't matter what anyone else did or said; *you* messed up and brought this on yourself." After I hung up on her, vowing never to speak to her again, I entertained the thought that she might have been right. Could it be true that my actions and no one else's caused this outcome? Impossible, I thought. But when I let my imagination float to all the troubled situations of my past, and looked from the perspective my friend suggested, it was getting harder to keep holding fast to the untrue idea that others caused anything to happen. No one besides myself was sabotaging me. How old were you when you learned this valuable lesson? The earlier a person realizes that their own actions have created their circumstances, the easier life becomes. I talk to many

older folks who haven't learned that their choices have something to do with the problems in front of them. You can spot them easily; they're the ones taking a victim's role in their life. Switching once again with

13. **Death**, which is the time in our lives where we learn that everything has a season. Events, people, projects, and life itself begin and end as time marches on. Death says it's time for the old to pass away to make room for the new. If a relationship has come to a natural ending, then a compete break from each other should be encouraged. We learn how painful grief is; however, this pain does stop hurting, whereas the pain of staying in a situation that needs to die never seems to stop. The end of a relationship season has no chance of resurrecting unless all involved move away and each becomes sovereign again. Only then, when both are on the other side of the pain and able to view the past with well-adjusted eyes, can a reunion ever have a chance to take hold. They will not be resurrecting the old but will be starting as new people discovering new things about each other. After the difficult lesson of Death, our hero, our Fool, you, we learn how to self-regulate our emotional investments with the outside world.

14. **Temperance** teaches how to stay centered, even if it means pretending to be balanced and grounded for a while before you get the hang of it. This is the first time we get to practice having a peace-filled heart and mind during a time of crisis and chaos. Temperance teaches us that nothing happening on the outside needs to affect how we feel on the inside. Life has gotten so fractious that, all of a sudden, Temperance fills our hearts with grace and our minds instantly become clear. Think back when life on the outside suggested extreme highs and lows, but you had no opinion, good or bad, about the event. You had absolutely no desire to participate with people who were calling you in to join in the disorder. You can be sure it was Temperance enlightening you to the fact that you can be in the world but not of it. We, as world travelers, are beginning to understand and enjoy true mastery in our own lives.

15. **The Devil** isn't something that starts on the outside, however. The Devil reveals our obsessions, compulsions, and destructive habits that each of us has created, and has an active presence inside us. This is where rage, conflict, enjoyment, defensiveness, a desire to control others, and self-harm are buried. Being conscious of your Devils helps tremendously. Eckhart Tolle, in the bestselling book titled *The Power of Now*, calls this the pain body. As we discover at very

young ages, life hurts in so many ways that we call in certain Devils to *help us cope* while we endure life's harsh experiences. This pain body represented by the Devil card was called in while you were young and had no power. Stuffing our rage when young kept us from harsh reprimand from others who were expressing their Devils. Keeping our rage quiet in the face of injustice kept us safe at the time. However, continuing to need our protective Devils into adulthood means they have taken up residency and are delighted with the destruction they can cause in our lives. Devils, our obsessive sabotaging habits, helped us cope when we were kids, but are holding us back as adults. Recognize the Devils' service, bless it, and release it every time they show up, making it harder for them to take hold. Being the observer of our rage and fascination with conflict when first feeling the impulse will help move past it. Not recognizing the Devils' past service and giving it liberty in your adult life causes consequences, most often immediate and severe. The traditional interpretation of the

16. **Tower** is sudden unwelcomed change, which terrifies everyone, of course. It's not in our nature as a species to enjoy change, let alone unwanted and unexpected change. However, if our Fool child had listened to the whispers of the previous card (addressing your obsessive compulsive behavior), then a complete destruction of beliefs and misunderstandings could have been avoided. It's been my experience that the Tower is more of a signal to get rid of ideas, theories, and opinions that don't measure up to who you are today. If reading the Tower as traditionally taught, as often as that card appears in readings, life would feel very unstable and risky. It is a serious card, and it would be wise for Fool to listen to its suggestions of dismantling inflexible beliefs, so life won't feel inclined to shock you to attention. The rest of the journey toward the World card is pretty easy. The journey we are all taking together here in this last chapter, from innocents to experienced, has held lots of Earth lessons, some very hard indeed. But now, as we pay attention and have been good students, we are on the other side of this mountain. We can now enjoy

17. **Star** of hope and spiritual connection, followed by

18. **Moon**, where we learn when to speak and when not to. We know what to reveal and what to keep safe inside. Fool graduates to a higher intuitive vibration plus creativity, so you are able to tell the story and write down what you have learned. Moon quietly shows the way to that awareness.

19. **The Sun** speaks much louder and shares messages of light and clarity. Solutions to all problems are revealed, analyzed with clear thinking and categorized on where the lessons are placed so nothing is forgotten.

20. **Judgment** has us enjoying the harvest from the field we planted way back at the beginning, when you and I were young, innocent, and without a care in the world. Speaking of

21. **The World**, we are triumphant, successful, and exuberant, since this card signals a job well done. Our Hero, Our Fool—You and I stand as well-prepared citizens of the world, with the wind at our backs and enough experience to do good work. We can rest in balance and wholeness from this long expedition from innocence to enlightenment. The last card in the deck, the 78th voucher to knowledge, offers congratulations for a job well done.

Conclusion

I'm passionate about teaching others how to serve people who are challenged by a situation and need competent counsel to get them out of the pain and relieve the stress of uncertainty. Sharing a person's most probable future trajectory takes away some surprises, lowers anxiety, and encourages certain action to be able to change course, to ease through a challenge with less suffering. Either way, you are empowering another with good information from the good company of the higher frequencies. With sincerity of purpose, I hope you find as much satisfaction in your life as I have in mine, helping others in this way. I hope you've enjoyed learning about the Tarot and all the different combinations, crosses, and reversals. I've redefined some of the meanings through my clients' feedback and critiques. The combinations I put in this book work for me as described. It's amazing the amount of information the Tarot can give you in a session. As you must have experienced by now, not every card in a reading is meant to be shared with the client. Some information on the table is for you, the advisor, informing you *about* your client and their situation so you can better support them.

I look forward to your continued interest and success with this wonderful divination tool. You can get a jump-start to understanding the Tarot by taking my video course at training.growyourlight.com. *The Clarity Tarot* deck is available on Amazon. I have live practice sessions available online to answer your questions. If interested in developing your individual style of awesome readings, subscribe to my email newsletter and *write a note saying you are interested in practicing live*, and I will notify you when classes are available.

With deep respect for your path,

Debra Zachau

At any one time,

you are someone's teacher or student.

The trouble begins when you assume

which one you are.

—Debra Zachau